The Complete Chi's Sweet Home

Part 2

Konami Kanata

contents

homemade 57~110+ +

homemade 57: a cat prepares

HIKKOSHI
HIKKOSHI
MEW
WHAT IS THIS?
HIKKOSHI
MEW
WHAT'S EVERY-ONE DOING?

I'M SO GLAD WE FOUND A NEW APARTMENT.
WE REALLY LUCKED OUT.
THERE
YEAH!
YOO-HOO!
MIYA
DASH
GRIP
MIYA
CHI WANTS TO PLAY TOO!
PLUCK
NO CLIMBING IN BOXES, CHI.
MYA
WHAT WAS THAT FOR, DADDY?
GRIP

OH!
SKEE SKEE
HIKKOSHI
NO, CHI!
WHOOSH
MYA
NOW LET'S PACK THIS STUFF.
I'LL HELP!
YEAH!
HEY?
HIKKOSHI
HIKKOSHI
MEOW
BUT CHI WAS PLAYING!
MYA
THERE ARE MORE OVER HERE.
CHI'S GONNA PLAY HERE, THEN.
MIYA
SKEE SKEE SKEE
HIKKOSHI
MEOW
OHH!

WOAH!
OOH!
AH!
HELP ME!!
MIA MIA
MEOW MEOW
HMM?
SOUNDS LIKE CHI'S CRYING SOME-WHERE.
MEOW MEOW MEOW MEOW MEOW
HIKKOSHI
HUH?
WHAT'S UP?
HELP!
MIA MIA
MII
HEY, WHAT ARE YOU UP TO?
HAH—

HEY
?
HIKKOSHI
MYA
AND WHAT'S THIS?
SKEE
SKEE
MEOW
OH
DFF
DFF
DFF
DFF
SNAG
FWUMP
SO SOFT!
PHEW,
LOOKS LIKE WE'RE FINALLY DONE WITH THAT ROOM.
DAD,
CHI'S MISSING.
HIKKOSHI
HIKKOSHI

SHE'S GONE.
HIKKOSHI
NO WAY!
WHERE IS CHI?
CHI!
PEEL PEEL PEEL
YOU IN THERE?
PEEL PEEL
OH!
ZZZ
CHI!
ZZZZ
YOU MUST BE JOKING.
ZZZZ
OK, WE CAN'T HAVE HER SNEAKING AROUND.
HUH?
YANK

SLAM
MEOW
WHAT'S GOWING ON?
SKFF SKFF SKFF
CHI WANTS TO PLAY IN THAT ROOM, TOO!
MEOW
LEMME OUT!
MEOW
SKFF SKFF SKFF SKFF SKFF
ALL RIGHT! NOW LET'S PICK UP THE PACE AND PACK OUR BAGS!
YEAH
SKFF SKFF SKFF
MEOW
SKFF SKFF SKFF SKFF
MEOW
SKFF
RATTL RATTL RATTL
THUMP THUMP
RATTL
SQUEEK
KLAK KLAK KLAK
SHUMP SHUMP
ALL CLEAR, CHI. YOU CAN COME OUT NOW.
MEOW
YAY, NOW CHI CAN PWAY IN THE ROOM!
DASH—
WE'RE GONNA MOVE TO A NEW HOME WITH YOU!
TO A PLACE WHERE WE CAN LIVE WITH CATS.

KREEP KREEP
HIKKOSHI
POKE
HIKKOSHI
HIKKO
WOBBL
WOBBL
WOBBL
WOBBL
HIKKOSHI
KOSHI
HIKKOS
LOOKS LIKE A PRE-MOVE PANIC TO ME.
LITTLE FLUS-TERED?
WHERE IS THIS PWACE!
MEOWR
ISN'T IT GREAT, CHI?

the end

homemade 58: a cat imagines

HIKKOSHI
THIS ISN'T CHI'S HOME?
IT'S MY HOME, BUT...
DID YOU PUT CHI AWAY?
KNOCK KNOCK
THANKS FOR COMING!
YUP
DASH
IT'S NOT MY HOME, BUT IT IS...
IS BUT ISN'T?
ISN'T BUT IS?

.........?
CONFUSED
DASHH
STOMP STOMP
YIKES!
ZING
STOMP STOMP
FOOTSTEPS?
STOMP STOMP STOMP STOMP
SO MANY FOOTSTEPS?
LET'S START WITH THIS ROOM.
SOUNDS GOOD.
STOMP STOMP
SO MANY FEET?
SO MANY!
STOMP STOMP STOMP
...
WHAM
KYAA
BING

BIG FOOT STEPS?
BIG FEET?
BIG FEET?
...
SORRY
IT'S HEAVY AND BIG, LET'S TAKE IT APART.
STMP
STMP
STMP
BANG BANG
BAN
TOK TOK TOK
IT IS OR ISN'T CHI'S HOME BUT IT'S BEING ATTACKED!
BOING
BOING
BOING
BOING
STMP STMP
THMP
THMP

AND SUDDENLY EVERYTHING'S ALL GONE.
YEAH
THERE'S NO-THING LEFT.

HMM ?
TUG TUG
I USED TO...
ROLL
LIE AROUND WITH CHI HERE.
YES, AND MOM WAS SHOCKED ...
WHEN SHE FIRST MET THE BEAR-CAT OVER HERE.
I HAD THE VACUUM.
FOOM

AND I GAVE HER HER FIRST TASTE
OF MILK OVER HERE.
GLUP GLUP
MILK
STARE
LAP LAP LAP
CHI!
YOU CAN COME OUT NOW.
MEOWR
WHAT ABOUT THE BIG BAD THING?

PEEK
IS IT HERE?
WHERE'D IT GO?
CHI'S BEEN HERE JUST A BIT
BUT SO MANY THINGS HAVE HAPPENED.
SLINK
SLINK
SLINK
SLINK
SLINK
YANK YANK
TREMBL
TREMBL

NOTHING'S LEFT HERE,
BUT SO MUCH IS TOO!
YEAH
THANK GOODNESS, THE BIG BAD THING IS GONE.
HEY?
WE'RE HEADING OUT TO OUR NEW HOME!
THE CAR'S WAITING.
MEOWR
EVERYTHING IS GONE!!

the end

homemade 59: a cat moves

WE'RE HERE AT LAST.
TWICH TWICH
TWICH
TWICH TWICH
TWICH TWICH

CHI HATES THIS BOX.
I ALWAYS GO TO BAD PLACES IN HERE.
WAHHH
TWITCH TWITCH TWITCH TWITCH
YAY
TMP TMP TMP
BI BI BI
OKAY OKAY
HUP HO HUP
WHAM
EEK
STOMP STOMP STOMP STOMP STOMP STOMP
THE BIG FEET ARE BACK?

STOMP STOMP STOMP
KYAA
SO MANY AGAIN?
!
NO WAY
NO WAY
NO WAY...
PWEASE NO
MIYA
STOMP
MIYA
STOMP
STOMP
STO...
STOMP
STOMP
STOMP
STOMP
STOMP
THANKS SO MUCH!

PHEW
WELL WELL
ALL THAT'S LEFT IS CHI.
HERE COMES CHI.
YO
COME OUT, CHI!
POP
HUSH
HMM?
COME, CHI.
MEOW
NO NO!
MEOW
NO PWEASE ...

HIKKOSHI
HAH?
THE WEIRD THING'S GONE?
THIS ISN'T A BAD PLACE?
SNFF SNFF SNFF
SNFF SNFF SNFF

...
THEN
WHERE AM I?
COME, CHI!
YOINK
KLAK KLAK
KLAK KLAK KLAK
HUH ?!
?!
KLAK KLAK
ISN'T THIS GREAT? YOUR OWN DOOR, CHI.
KLAK KLAK
PUSH
TRY IT.
MIYAR
WHAT-CHA DOING, DADDY ?!
MEOWR

YO-ZY
CHECK THIS OUT!
?!
HUH?
YOUR OWN STEPS.
MIYA!!
LEMME DOWN!
AND WE HAVE A YARD TOO!
YO-ZY
AH!
!
...
ARE YOU GLAD, CHI?
PANT
PANT
...

SO CHI ...
THIS IS OUR NEW HOME.
DO YOU LIKE IT?
WE MOVED HERE FOR YOU, CHI.
SIGH
ALL RIGHT, LET'S GO HOME NOW.
MIYA
HIKKOSHI

the end

homemade 60: a cat sniffs

I DON'T KNOW THIS PWACE.
...
MIYA MIYA
EVERYONE, LET'S GO HOME!
PEEL PEEL
SHFL SHFL
...?

KRR
KRR
KRR
SNFF
SNFF
I DON'T KNOW THIS SMELL.
SNFF
SNFF
I DON'T KNOW THESE SMELLS.
DADDY'S SMELL.
SNFF
SNFF
SNFF
AHH
MIYA
OH, CHI!
LET'S GO HOME DADDY.
MYA
LET'S GO.
ARE YOU HUNGRY?
THERE THERE
HEY?
WHERE'S THE CAT FOOD?
SHMP

...
PEEL
PEEL
PEEL
SNFF
SNFF
SNFF
DON'T KNOW THIS SMELL.
NOT THIS ONE EITHER.
SNFF
SNFF
SNFF
YOHEY'S SMELL.
SNFF
SNFF
AH
HAH
MIYA
OH
CHI.
YOHEY, LET'S GO HOME.

MIYA
LET'S GO HOME.
IF I SEE YOUR TOYS I'LL GIVE THEM TO YOU, OK?
DASH
HIKKOSHI
...
DON'T KNOW THIS SMELL.
SNFF SNFF SNFF
MOMMY'S SMELL.
SNFF SNFF SNFF
DON'T KNOW THIS SMELL, EITHER.
SNFF SNFF SNFF

AHH
FU
MY
LET'S GO HOME.
MIYA
IS IT POTTY TIME?
JUST A SEC!
WHERE'S THE LITTER KIT?
DASH
HIKKO
...
DRAT!

MOM, WHERE SHOULD I PUT THIS?
OVER THERE IS GOOD.
OVER WHERE?
MEW
MEW
MEW
MEW
SKFF
SKFF
SKFF
SKFF
LET'S GO HOME.
MIYAN
SKFF
SKFF
SKFF
SKFF
HERE.
THIS IS YOURS.
PLOP

MIYA
THAT'S NOT WHAT I WANT!
HOME, HOME!
MEOW
BOFF BOFF BOFF
HOME NOW!
MEOW
BOFF BOFF BOFF
HEY...

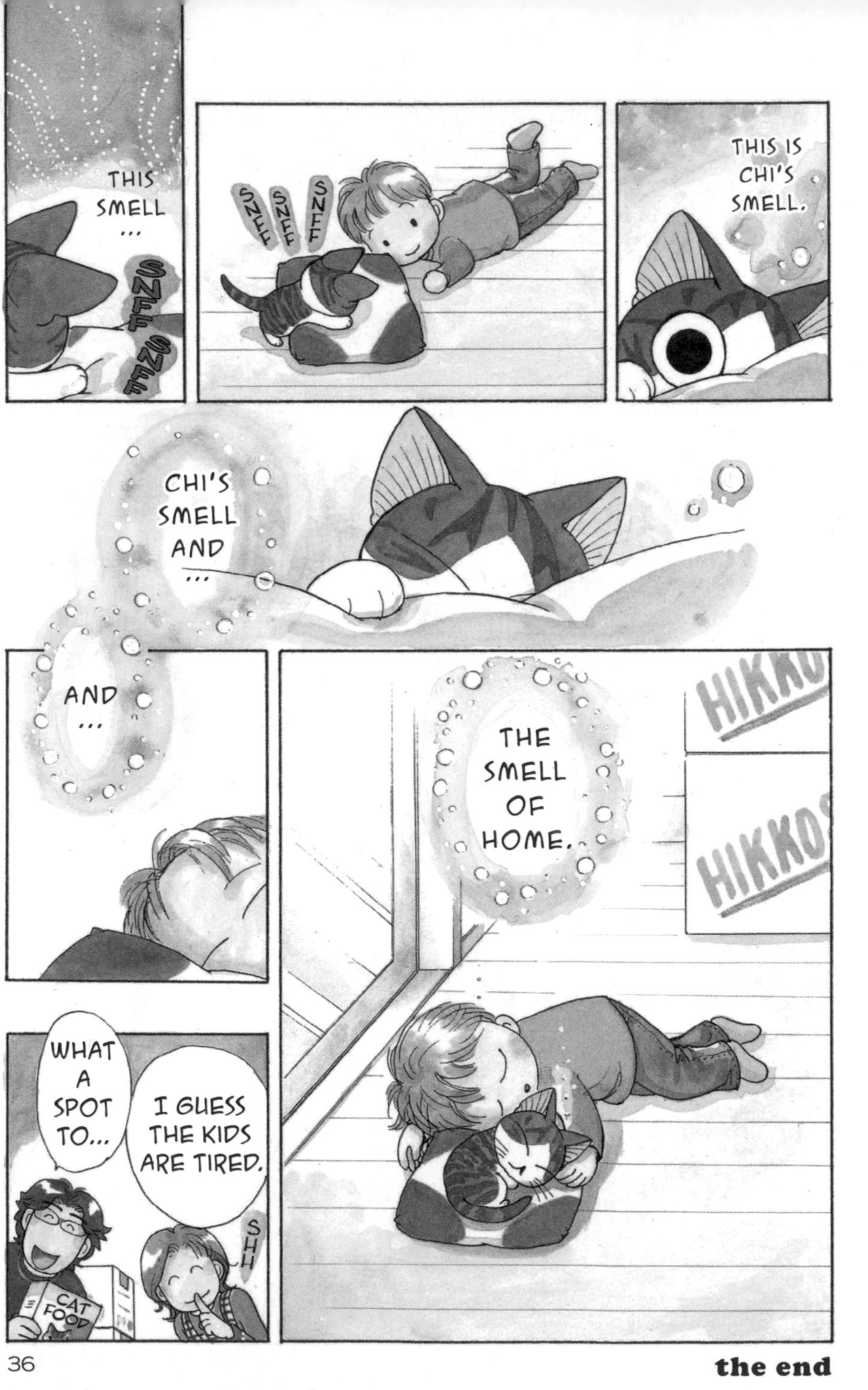
THIS SMELL ...
SNFF SNFF
SNFF SNFF SNFF
THIS IS CHI'S SMELL.
CHI'S SMELL AND ...
AND ...
THE SMELL OF HOME.
HIKKO
HIKKO
WHAT A SPOT TO...
I GUESS THE KIDS ARE TIRED.
SHH
CAT FOOD

the end

homemade 61: a cat cultivates

WHY AREN'T WE GOING HOME?
MEOW?
VOOM
WHY SO CAREFREE, YOU TWO?

HOME?
WHAT ABOUT HOME?
CALM DOWN AND THINK.
THIS IS CHI'S HOME.
SNFF SNFF
THIS IS NOT.
THIS IS CHI'S.
SNFF SNFF
BUT THIS IS NOT.
CHI'S
CHI'S!
CHI'S
CHI'S
NOT CHI'S
NOT CHI'S
NO
NOT CHI'S!

SKEFF
SKEFF
SKEFF
SKEFF
THE STWANGE PLACE AND CHI'S THINGS ARE
ALL MIXED UP!
WHAT IS THIS PLACE?

WHAT SHOULD CHI DO?
HRN?
HMM?
!
HO-HO
THIS IS MINE!
I'LL MAKE ALL THIS MINE!
TEEHEE

GRIP
RIP RIP RIP
MEW
THIS IS CHI'S NOW.
NUZZL
RUB RUB
MYA
THIS IS CHI'S!
MYA
THIS IS CHI'S TOO!
KSSH KSSH KSSH KSSH
SMAK
TWINGE TWINGE TWINGE TWINGE
GRIN
CHI'S STUFF.
MYA

RUB RUB
RUB
RUB
RUB
RUB
RUB
MYA
CHI'S STUFF!
ROLL ROLL
ROLL...
TAKE THIS! YOU'RE MINE!
MEOW
TAKE THAT AND THAT!
MIYA
THIS IS CHI'S TOO!
MIYA
PANT
PANT
PANT
PANT
PANT
PANT
SKAMPER...
PANT
PANT
PANT
PANT
PANT

ALL RIGHT!
IT'S ALL CHI'S NOW!
MIYA
MOM, I'M GOING TO DAD'S ROOM!

TMP
TMP
TMP
UH?
TMP
TMP
TMP
!
TMP
TMP
STILL MORE PWACES THAT AREN'T CHI'S?
MEOWR
TMP
TMP
TMP
TMP

the end

homemade 62: a cat climbs

SNFF
SNFF
SNFF

CHI DOESN'T KNOW THIS SMELL.
SNFF
SNFF
SNFF
FWIP

SO MANY STWANGE STEP-STEPS!
CHI HAS TO INVESTIGATE!
HOP
FUMP
HOP
HUFF
HUFF
I HAVE CWIMBED LIKE THIS BEFORE.
HUFF
HUFF
RUN!

HUFF
HEE!
HUFF
HUFF
HUFF
HUFF
HUFF
HUFF
HUFF
BREAK TIME!
MY
LOOK AT YOU!
OOH!
STARE
LIKE THE STAIRS?
HUH?

CHI'S AS BIG AS MOMMY NOW!
WHOA-HO-HO!
FWIP
HOP
FLUMP
TWIRL
MYA
WOW!
I'M A LITTLE BIGGER THAN MOMMY!

CWIMB, CWIMB!
HOP
FUMP
SPIN
MIYA
WOAH!
I GUESS YOU'VE TAKEN TO THE STAIRS, HUH.
CHI'S BIG!!
HOP
HOP
CWIMB, CWIMB!
CWIMB, CWIMB!
HOP
PANT
PANT
PANT
PANT
PANT

FIP
CHI!
PANT
PANT
PANT
PANT
CHI'S HUGE!
MEOW
COME DOWN, CHI!
MEOW!
CHI'S AMAZING!
OH!

CHI LIKES THIS THING. IT'S CHI'S NOW.
RUB RUB
COME AND HAVE SOME MILK, CHI.
MIULK!!
MIULK! MIULK!
HONEY, YOHEI... I'VE GOT SOME SNACKS FOR YOU.
YAY!
OKAY
AH!
!
GULP

GO ON DOWN, YO-HEI.
OK!
TMP
TMP
TMP
HMM?
HUFF
HUFF
HUFF
HUFF
HELP ME!! I'M SCARED!!
MEOWR MEOWR MEOWR

the end

homemade 63: a cat greets

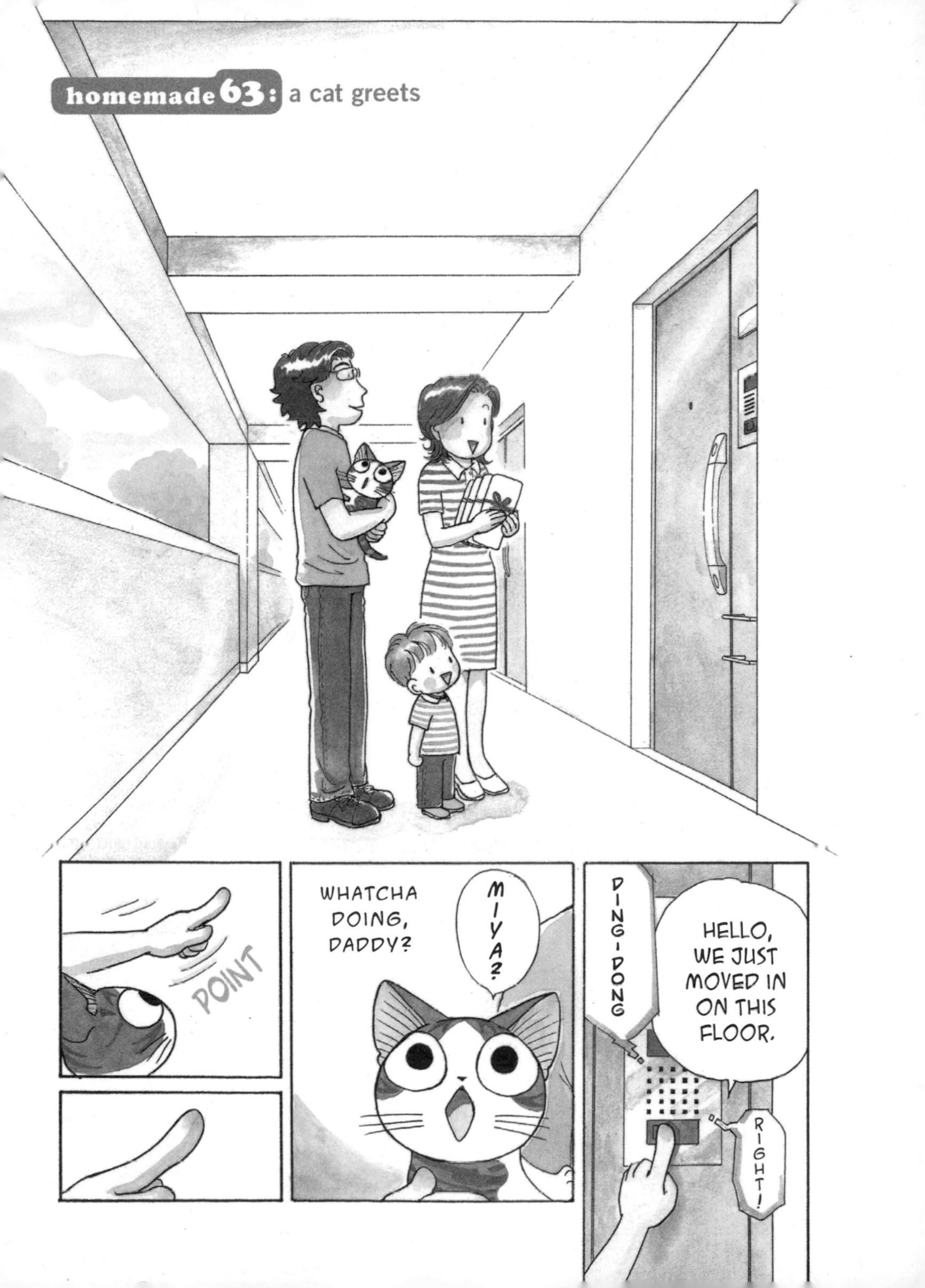

POINT
WHATCHA DOING, DADDY?
MIYA?
DING-DONG
HELLO, WE JUST MOVED IN ON THIS FLOOR.
RIGHT!

WE'RE THE YAMADAS.
WE MOVED HERE WITH THIS KIT-TEN.
PLEASED TO MEET YOU.
OH, A CAT?
AND WHAT ARE YOU?
MEOW
WOULD YOU LIKE TO SEE MY LITTLE ONE?
WAIT A SEC.
THUP THUP
YOU'RE MEETING NEW ANIMAL FRIENDS.
HOW FUN, YES?
WHAT NOW?
CHIRP
HERE WE ARE!
!
ISN'T SHE CUTE?
CHIRP

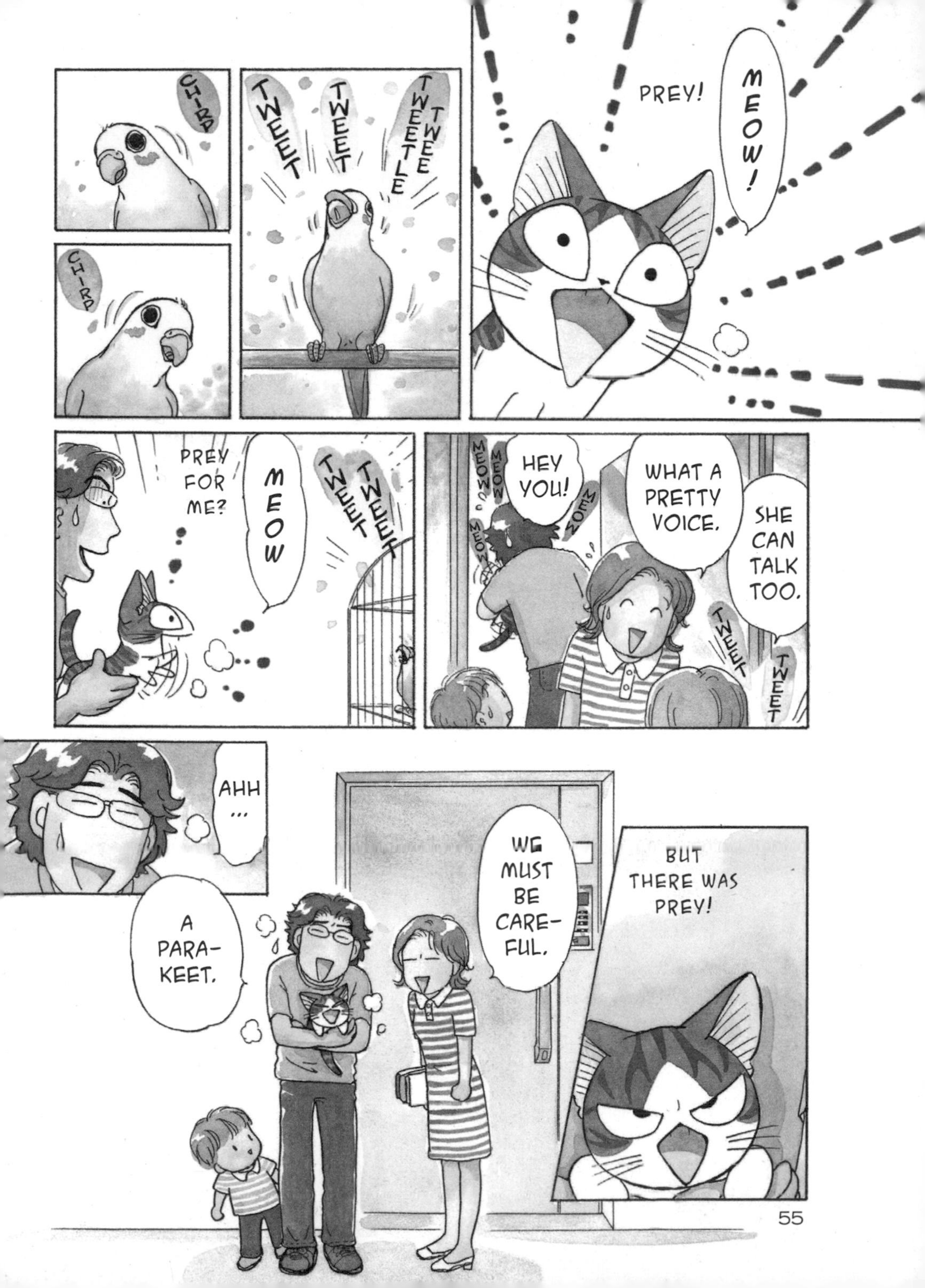
CHIRP
CHIRP
TWEET
TWEET
TWEETLE
TWEE
PREY!
MEOW!
PREY FOR ME?
MEOW
TWEET
TWEET
MEOW
MEOW
HEY YOU!
MEOW
MEOW
WHAT A PRETTY VOICE.
SHE CAN TALK TOO.
TWEET
TWEET
AHH ...
A PARAKEET.
WE MUST BE CAREFUL.
BUT THERE WAS PREY!

LET'S TRY NEXT DOOR.
NICE TO MEET YOU.
OH, YOU HAVE A KITTY AS WELL.
HUH?
YOU HAVE ONE TOO?
ALICE, COME OUT.
YOU'VE GOT A COMRADE.
THEY HAVE A CAT!
I HOPE YOU BECOME FRIENDS, CHI.

MIYA
WHAT ARE YOU?
NOD
NYAHN
HOW DO YOU DO?
"...I DO?"
NOD
I CAN'T BELIEVE THEY'RE THE SAME SPECIES.

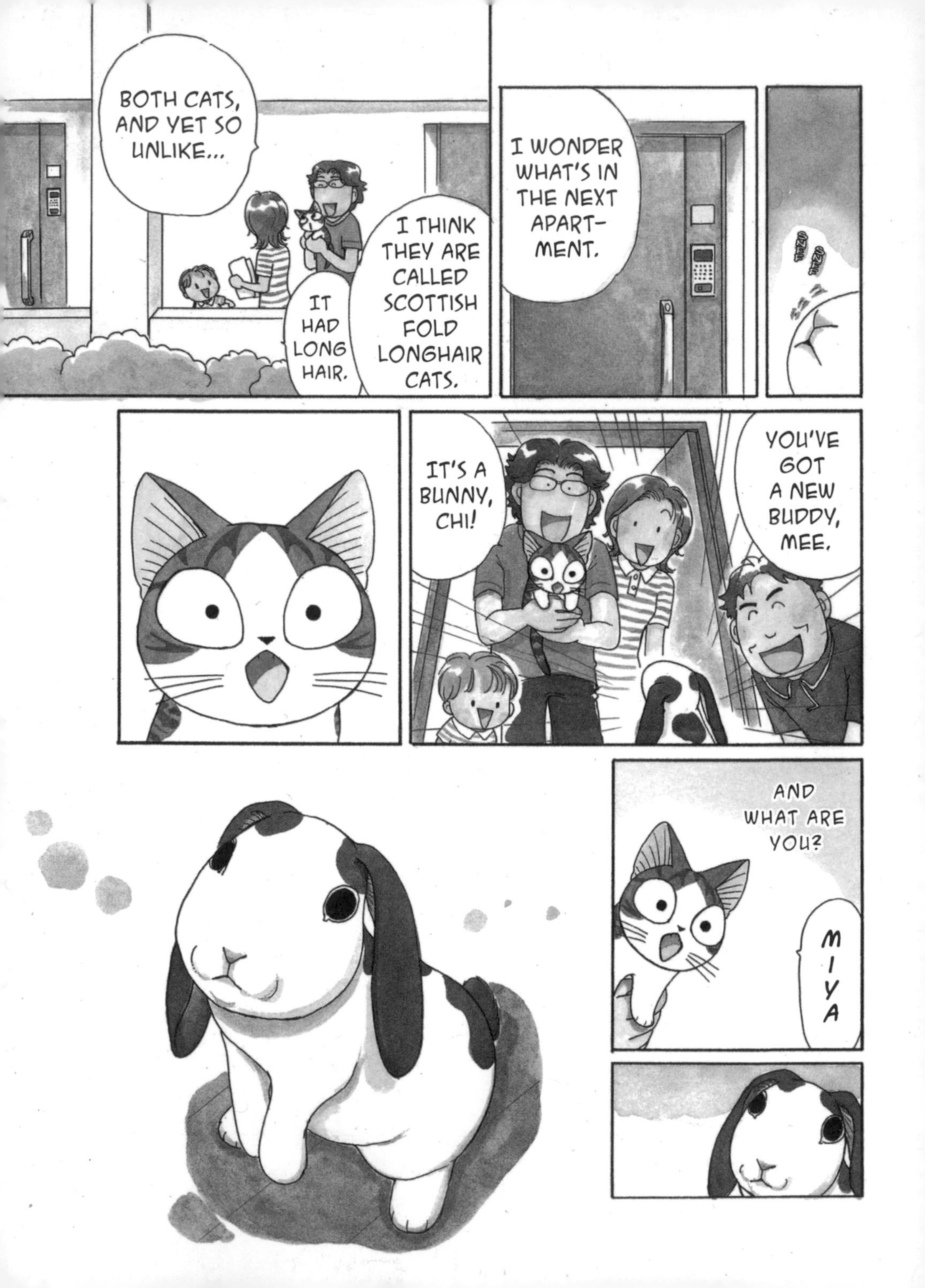
I WONDER WHAT'S IN THE NEXT APARTMENT.
BOTH CATS, AND YET SO UNLIKE...
I THINK THEY ARE CALLED SCOTTISH FOLD LONGHAIR CATS.
IT HAD LONG HAIR.
YOU'VE GOT A NEW BUDDY, MEE.
IT'S A BUNNY, CHI!
AND WHAT ARE YOU?
MIYA

MIYA
WHAT ARE YA?
MEOW
WHAT ARE YA?!
MEOW
REALLY, WHAT ARE YA?
HUFF
MUP
MIYAN
NO RESPONSE.
SHFF SHFF SHFF
BUNNIES SURE ARE QUIET.
NO CRYING FROM THEM.
WE'VE GOT OUR NEXT DOOR NEIGHBOR LEFT.

I WONDER WHAT THEY HAVE?
OH!
WUF
WUF
I KNOW!
WUF
WUF
WUF
WUF
THIS ONE'S TOO EASY.
WUF
WUF
WUF
!
MIYAN
CHI DOESN'T LIKE THIS ONE!

the end

homemade 64: a cat challenges

WUF WUF
THEY HAVE A DOG!
KUSANO
SO THERE'S A DOG NEXT DOOR.
HUFF
HUFF
DING-DONG
NO WAY

IT'S JUST ME NOW...
MOM'S OUT SHOP-PING.
Yamada
HUH?
THE BARKER ISN'T HERE.
WE'RE THE YAMADAS. WE MOVED HERE
WITH A KITTY.
SEE YOU THEN.

AND THE DOG?
TUG TUG
DOG?
OH, HE'S HERE!
HEY, DAVID!
WHAM
DASH
RUFF
WHAT!
HUFF
SCAMPER
SCAMPER
RUF-RUFF
HUFF
SCAMPER
SCAMPER
RUF-RUFF
RUF-RUFF
RUFF
HUFF
WOAH!

SAY HI, CHI.
LOOK, DAVID, A NEW FRIEND.
TUMP
SNUFF
SNUFF
SNUFF
SNUFF
HE'S SNIFFING MY SMELL!
FSSK
WHO SAID YOU COULD?
RUFF

WHAT'S THE MAT-TER?
HE WANTS TO PLAY.
HUH?
RUF-RUFF
RU-RUFF
RUFF
HSSS
WHAT?
SMR SMR
OH, CHI!
NO!!!
!

HEEL!
DAVID, LAY DOWN.
DOWN.
STILL
MYA
WHAT'S UP?
STIFF

SWOOP
MIYA
WHAT'S THE MATTER?
PAT PAT
STIFF
DOGS ARE AMAZING!
REALLY!
STILL
MYA
WHAT'S UP, HUH?
SWFF SWFF SWFF
MIYA
LICK LICK LICK
WHATCHA DOING?
MEOW
WHAT'S UP WITH YOU, HUH?
BLEH

HUFF
HUFF
HUFF
PANT
...
DAVID SURE IS A LITTLE SMARTY.
CHI COULD NEVER DO THAT!
GOOD BOY
WUFF WUFF
WEIRDO

the end

homemade 65: a cat worries

IS THIS THE SPOT?
TAP
...TAP TAP TAP

IS HERE GOOD?
TAP TAP TAP
SHE SEEMS LOST.
HER WHOLE WORLD HAS CHANGED SINCE THE MOVE.
CHI SEEMS A LITTLE TENSE.

IS HERE GOOD?
IS CHI GOOD HERE?
PAT
I HOPE YOU COME TO LIKE YOUR NEW HOME, CHI.
MYA
HUH?
PET PET

PET PET
PET PET
PRRRR PRRRR
PRRRR PRRRR
OH?

HERE...
I'M JUST FINE, HERE!
HAH
YAWN
LOOKS LIKE CHI'S ASLEEP.
SHE'S SETTLED IN AT LAST.
IT WAS A BIT HECTIC...
WE'RE ALL A LITTLE TIRED.

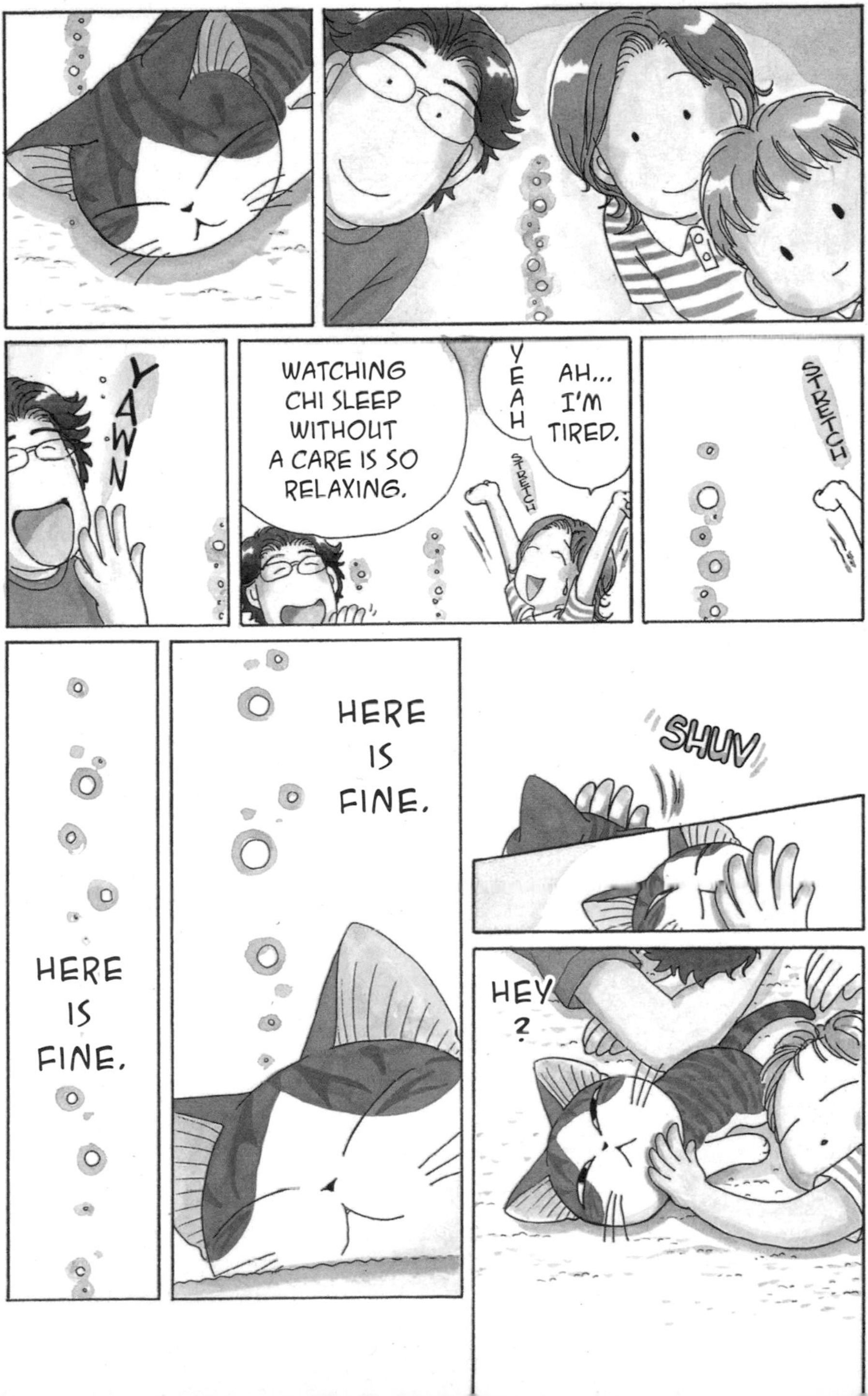
YAWN
WATCHING CHI SLEEP WITHOUT A CARE IS SO RELAXING.
YEAH
AH... I'M TIRED.
STRETCH
STRETCH
HERE IS FINE.
HERE IS FINE.
SHUV
HEY?

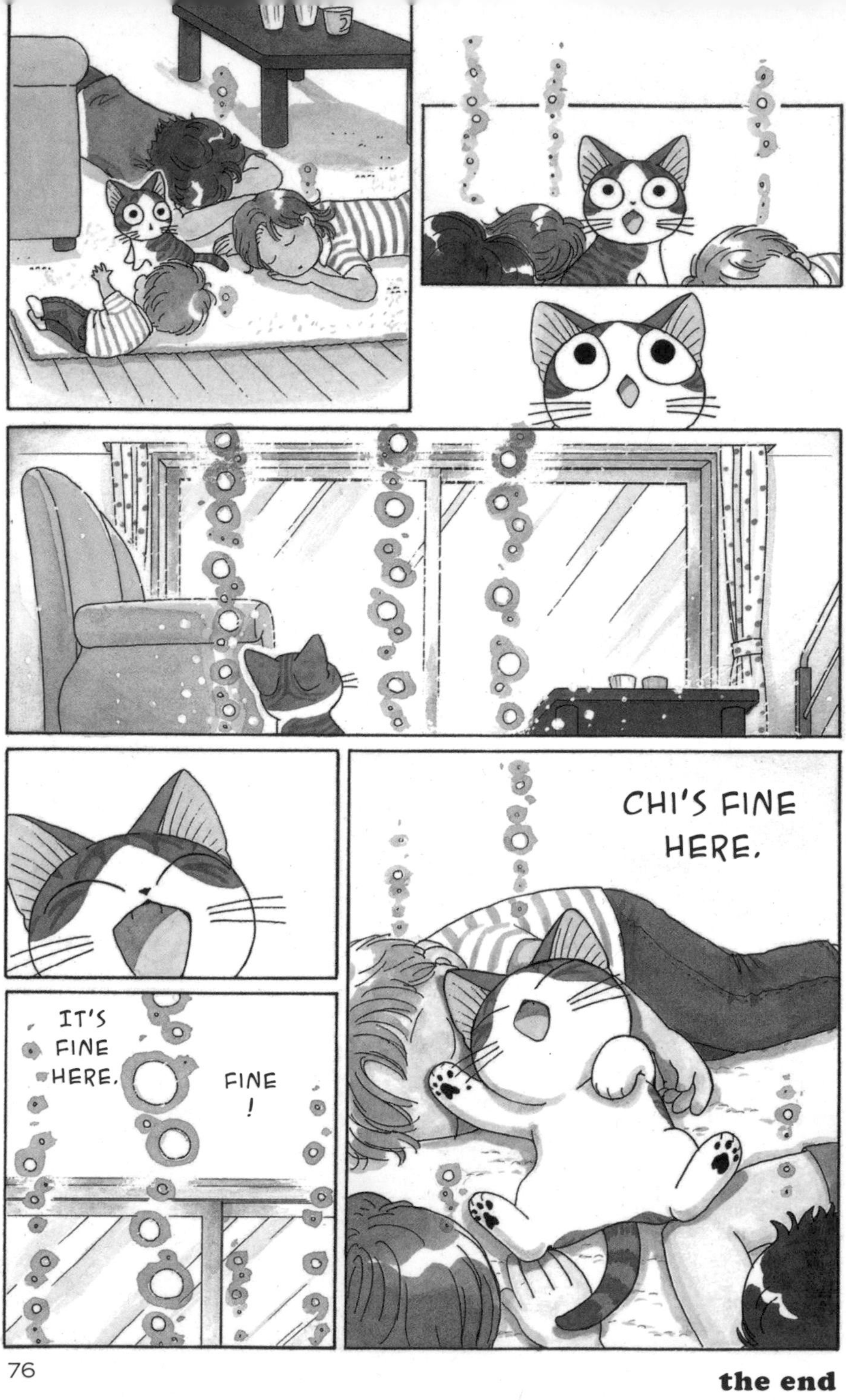
CHI'S FINE HERE.
IT'S FINE HERE.
FINE !

the end

homemade 66: a cat is mistaken

RIP
RIP
SHFF
SHFF
RSTL RSTL
RSTL...
MIYA
DADDY, WHAT'S THAT?

TA-DAH
IT'S A NAIL BOARD FOR CHI.
CHI CAN USE IT TO WEAR DOWN HER CLAWS.
ISN'T IT COOL, CHI?
MIYA
YAY!
RUSTLE

RUSTLE
RUSTLE
RUSTLE
RUSTLE
MIYA
THIS IS GREAT!
HUH?
MYA?
YOINK
HEY?
MYA?
SNIP
THERE
PLOP
THAT'S CHI'S NOW.

WHAT'S THIS?
SHFT
SHFT
GRIN
MEOW
THIS IS PRETTY NICE!
CHI'S RELAXING.
THAT'S NOT WHAT IT'S FOR.
GRIP

SKRRCH
SKRRCH
FILE YOUR CLAWS, CHI.
SKRRCH
SKRRCH
SEE.
WHAT?
MYA?
SKRRCH
SKRRCH
SKRRCH
CLEAN.
LICK LICK LICK
SHE'S LICKING YOU.
UH.
LICK
THAT'S NOT IT.

SNATCH
SNATCH
HEY!
CHI'S CLAWS ...
WHAT?!
SQUEEN
SKRRCH
WHAT!
CAN BE FILED ON THIS.
MEOW
WHATCHA DOING TO ME?!
DO YOU GET IT NOW, CHI?

SWAP
MEOW
DON'T YOU
EVER GRAB
MEOWR
MEOWR
CHI'S PAWS!
SLASH
OUCH!

MY! SHE REALLY GOT YOU.
CLAWS!
WHAT NEXT...
Cat Care
I GUESS WE BETTER CLIP HER CLAWS THEN.
I GUESS SO.
IT SAYS SQUEEZE HER PAW PADS TO EXTEND HER CLAWS.
HMM
REALLY?
Cat Care
HEY...
HEY?!
GLARE

the end

homemade 67: a cat has her claws trimmed

Cat Care
OKAY, CHI!
WHAT A GOOD KITTY.
WHAT'S UP DADDY?

PRESS THE TOE-PAD TO EXTEND THE CLAW.
Cat Care
GOT IT!
BUT I'M A LITTLE TENSE.
GRAB
SQUEEZE
MEOW
WHATCHA DOING, DADDY?
HEY?

MEOWR
EEP!
UH, CHI, DON'T MOVE!
MEOW
WHAT IS THAT?
MEOW
WHAT ARE YOU UP TO?
GADE
MEOW
NOS!
MEOW
NO!
GADE
STOP FIDGETING. I CAN'T TRIM YOUR CLAWS.
HOLD HER DOWN!
HOLD!
MIYA
MIYA
SMUSH
SMUSH
MEOW
LEMME GO!
SHOOSH

UM
UH
STAY STILL, CHI!
MEOW
LET ME GO!
SWID SWID
MIYA
LET ME GO!
SWID SWID
YOU SHOULD ONLY CUT THE CLEAR EDGE?
THE BOOK SAYS IF YOU CUT THE COLORED PART,
IT WILL
BLEED
BLEED!
THERE'S BLEEDING?!

IT'S NO USE.
I'M TOO AFRAID NOW.
SWIP SWIP SWIP
SWIP SWIP SWIP
WAH!
KICK KICK KICK
HUFF HUFF
LET ME GO!
MEOWR
GRAB
GRAB
OH?!

NOW BE GOOD, CHI.
!
WHA-!
WHATCHA DOING TO ME?!
MIYA
GRR
SNIP

YEAH, DAD GOT ONE!
YUP,
ONE CLAW.
GRRRR
GRRRR
THAT HURTS.
GRRRR
GRRRR
SNIP
OWWIE
SNIP
SNIP
CHI'S MAD.
SNIP
SNIP
SNIP
Care

AH
THAT WAS ROUGH,
BUT NONE OF HER CLAWS BLED.
STILL ...
DASH—
CHI
...
PISSED

the end

homemade 68: a cat joins in

TIME TO DIG IN!
MYA
IT'S GOOD!
OH?

??
MIYA
YOHEY, YOHEY
MIYA
WHAZ-ZAT?
HRN?
SOMETHING TASTY?
MEOW
THIS?
IT'S A SPOON.
SNIF SNIF SNIF

AH
WHAT A TASTY SMELL.
MIYA
JUST THE SMELL?
CHOMP
THAT CUSTARD TURNED OUT TASTY, NO?
MUNCH MUNCH
MIYA
MOMMY MOMMY
WHAZZAT?
MIYA
HUH?
THIS?
MIYA
IS IT TASTY?
IS IT?

HAVE A BIT.
SNIF SNIF SNIF
MUNCH MUNCH MUNCH
MEOW
TASTY!
WANT SOME, CHI?
IT'S GOOD!

MUNCH MUNCH MUNCH
LICK LICK
MEOW
SO TASTY!
!
THERE...
IS A MOUNTAIN OF GOODIES!

TASTY
YUM-O
UH-HUH
MUNCH
CHOMP
CHEW
TEE HEE
YOO HOO
HA HA HA
CHI WANTS TO FEAST TOO.
MIYA
MEOW
STILL WANT MORE, HUH?
MAYBE SHE WANTS TO CLIMB UP HERE.
MEOW
FEAST!!
WE SHOULDN'T HAVE FED HER PEOPLE FOOD.
FEAST!!
MEOW
NO!

MIYA
MEOW
CHI WANTS TO FEAST!
MEOW MEW MEOW
WHAT CAN YOU DO...
LET'S TRY THIS.
KLAK
KLAK
PLOP
WOAH

MEOW
HERE YOU GO, CHI.
TUNK
WOW!
MYA
LET'S DIG IN!
I PUT CHI'S ON THE TABLE, TOO!
MEOW
WHAT A FEAST!
IS IT TASTY, CHI?

the end

homemade 69: a cat plays in the yard

THE YARD!
YAY!
DASH
CHI!
ZING
!

ARE YOU MAD AT CHI?
IT'S OKAY?
SPROING
GO AHEAD. YOU CAN PLAY IN THIS YARD.
WE CAN LIVE HERE WITH YOU, SO PLAY WITH EASE, CHI.
VOOM

SNIF
SNIF
SNIF
SMELLS LIKE DADDY.
SMELLS LIKE YOHEY!
SNIF
SNIF
SNIF
SNIF
SNIF
SNIF
A NEW SMELL!
ISK
ISK
ISK
YAY!
FLOP
ROLL

THE NEW SMELL...
ROLL ROLL ROLL
IS NOW CHI'S!
CHEW CHEW
BLECH
ANOTHER NEW SMELL.
SNIF SNIF SNIF
THIS IS CHI'S TOO.
RUB RUB RUB RUB
MORE NEW SMELLS.
THIS IS ALL CHI'S.
RUB RUB RUB RUB
ANOTHER SMELL?
SNIF SNIF SNIF

HUH?
I KINDA KNOW THIS ONE.
WHAT IS IT?
SNIF
SNIF
SNIF
HMM ?
PANT
WOOF
MEOWR
EEK!

STAY OUT! THIS IS CHI'S PLACE!
MEOW
RUFF
RUFF
RUFF
OH?!
PANT
PANT
PANT
AH!
SHAK
CHI SAVED THE YARD!

BOING BOING
DART
BOING BOING
PANT
DART DART
HRN?
NOW WHAT?
PANT
BOING BOING
DART DART
PANT
WHAT IS IT?
SHOOP

WUF
BOING BOING
WOOF
DART
WHAT?
BOWOW
DART
DASH
HEY!

the end

homemade 70: a cat figures out

RUN AWAY!
MEOW!
ZASH
ZWASH
!

WOOF
MYA
RUN!
MEOW
DASH
DART
HUFF
HUFF
HUFF
HA
HEY, YOU SCARED ME.

WHERE'D HE GO?
TIP
TIP-A
TIP
TIP
WHERE?
WHOOSH
WOOF
WHOOSH
MYA
MEOW
RUN!
DASH
HEY?

GONE AGAIN.
WILL HE COME OUT AGAIN?
BUT
SNEAK SNEAK SNEAK
FOOSH
WOOF
MYA
HE'S BACK!
MEOW
DASH—
HOW DOES IT KNOW WHERE CHI IS?

DANGER-OUS!
HRM?
ZAK
A STWANGE SOUND.
ZAK
ZAK
SNIF SNIF SNIF
FROM HERE... STWANGE.
WOOF
MYA

FLOP
MYA
!
WOOF
WOOF
EEK! HE'S GONNA BWITE ME!
MEOW
FLAP FLAP FLAP
FLAP FLAP
FLAP FLAP FLAP
HUH ?

KYUUN
REACH
REACH
REACH
REACH
REACH
ARE YOU STUCK?
KYUUN
GRIN
MIYA
CHI FIGURED IT OUT!

MYA
CHI CAN GO THROUGH!
DASH—
MYA
BARKS CAN'T.
MYA
COME AND GET ME!
MIYA
MIYA
WOOF
MEOW
CHI'S AMAZING, HUH?
HMPH
LOOKS LIKE THE NEW TENANT IS AT DAVID'S LEVEL.
NYA
HMPH

the end

homemade 71: a cat hides out

DASH
RSTL
RSTL
RSTL
RSTL
MYA
SNATCH
WHAT ARE YOU DOING?

HA-HA
MIYA
YOU SCARED ME.
MYA
SPRING
DASH
RUN!
MIYA
?
DASH
DASH!
HUFF
HA
HUFF
HUFF

PEEK
HEY?
WHERE'D YOHEY GO?
CHI!
MEOW!
MYA
HA HA
YOU FOUND ME!
MEOW
DASH

HUFF
HUFF
HUFF
CHI
MIYA
THIS IS FUN!
CHI
HUH?

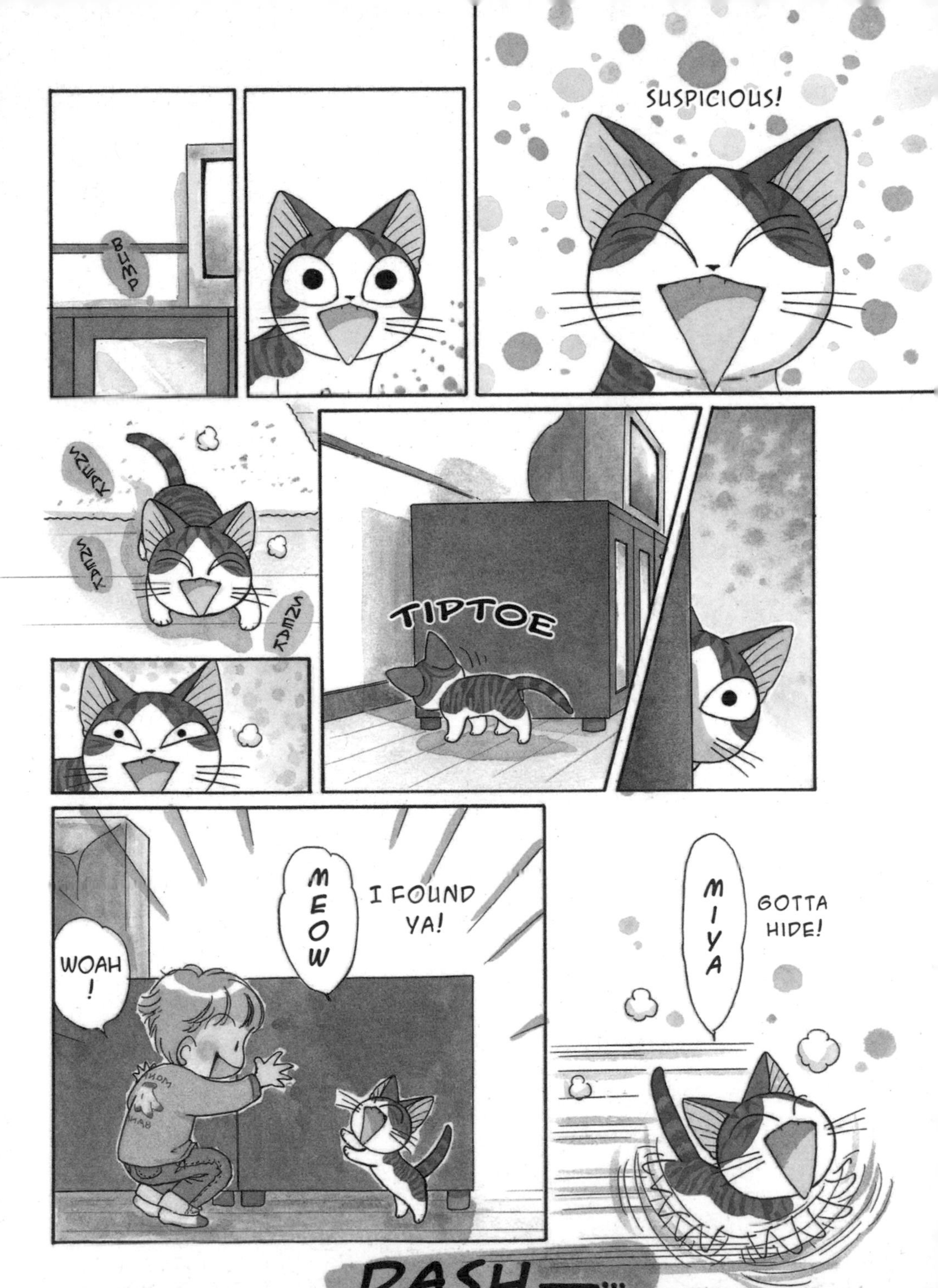
BUMP
SUSPICIOUS!
SNEAK
SNEAK
SNEAK
TIPTOE
I FOUND YA!
MEOW
WOAH!
GOTTA HIDE!
MIYA
DASH—...

DASH
MYA
YAY!
WHERE DO I HIDE?
SHUV SHUV
STICK
WHERE TO HIDE?
PLUNK
SLINK SLINK SLINK
I FOUND YOU.
PAT
FRMYA
YOU FOUND ME!
MYA

CHI!
HE-HEH
WHERE'D HE GO?
TIP
TIP
TIP
TIP
TIP
TIP
FLT
AH!
MYA
OH!
MIYA!
I FOUND YOHEY!
MEOW
CHI HIDES NEXT!
MYA
TIME TO HIDE!
BOUND

DASH—
HMM ...
DRY
CAT FOOD
NOPE.
WHERE WILL HE NOT FIND ME?
DASH—
FOUND IT!

the end

homemade 72: a cat hides out some more

POOF
HUFF
POOF
POOF
WHERE ARE YA HIDING, CHI?
HUFF
HUFF

MAYBE OVER HERE?
OVER HERE?
HMM?
GRIN
HOW ABOUT HERE?
THMP THMP THMP
PEEK
HUH?
!

NOT HERE.
EEP!
FLUSTER
TURN
THE DRESSER?
SLINK
SLINK
SLINK
HMM, NOT HERE.
MAYBE IN THAT PULLED DRAWER.
STILL

MONKEY BANANA
...
THMP THMP THMP
SHE'S NOT HERE EITHER.
FWAH
I DID IT!

NOT HERE.
NOT HERE EITHER.
WATER
PHEW
WATER
I'M THIRSTY.
WATER
GLUG GLUG GLUG
YOHEI, MOM'S HOME.
WANT
SOME FLAN?

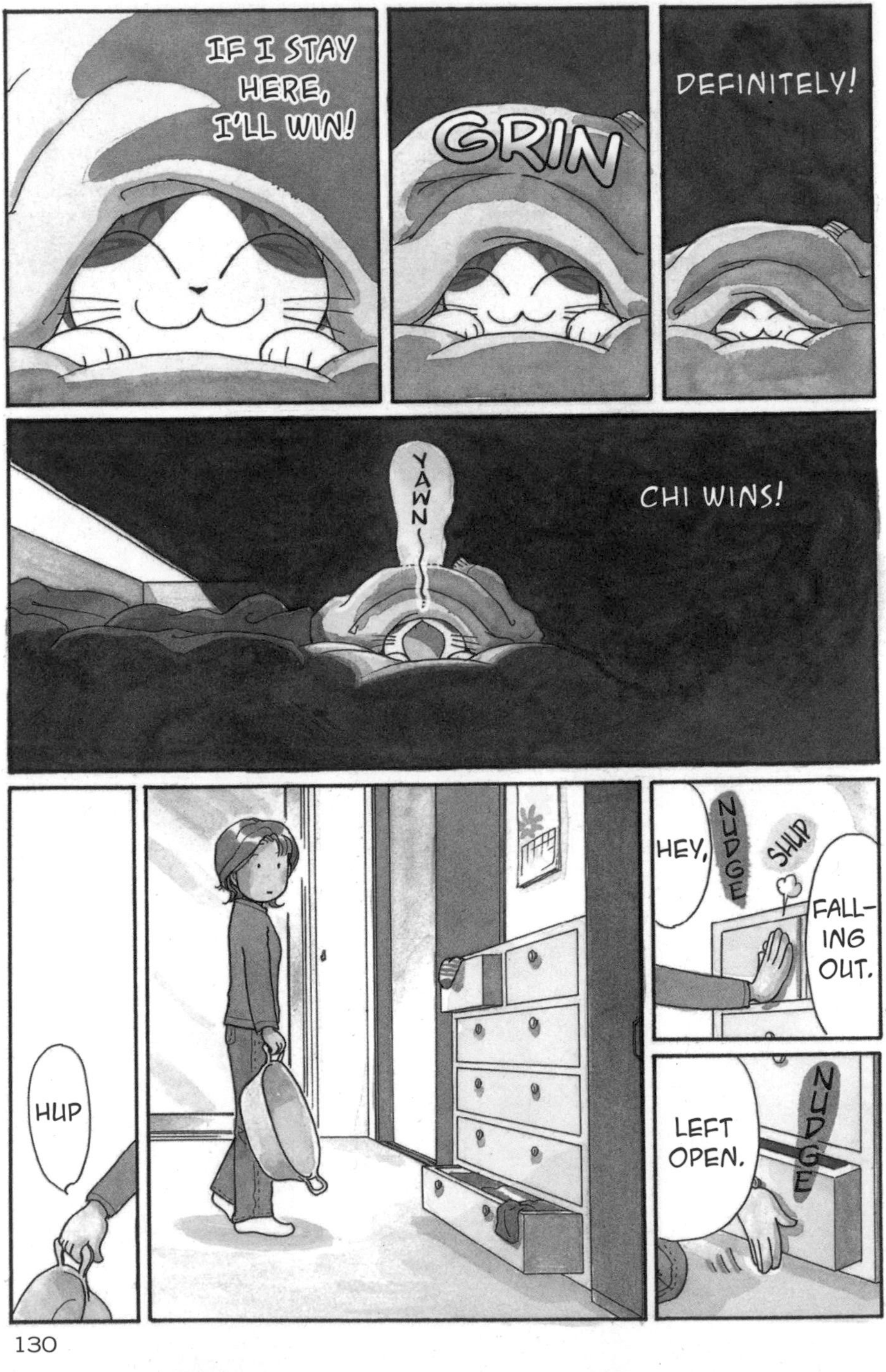
IF I STAY HERE, I'LL WIN!
GRIN
DEFINITELY!
YAWN
CHI WINS!
HUP
HEY,
NUDGE
SHUP
FALLING OUT.
LEFT OPEN.
NUDGE

SLID
I SEE.
ROGER THAT!
THUD
THUD
THUD
TWIST TWIST
TWIST
CHOP CHOP CHOP
SAY

WHERE'S CHI?
BEEP
CHI?
OH!
HMM ?
I DON'T KNOW...
ZZZ
MONKEY

the end

homemade 73: a cat is sought

CHI
CHI
CHI
CHI
CHI
NO REPLY.
WHERE IS CHI HIDING?
...
YAWN

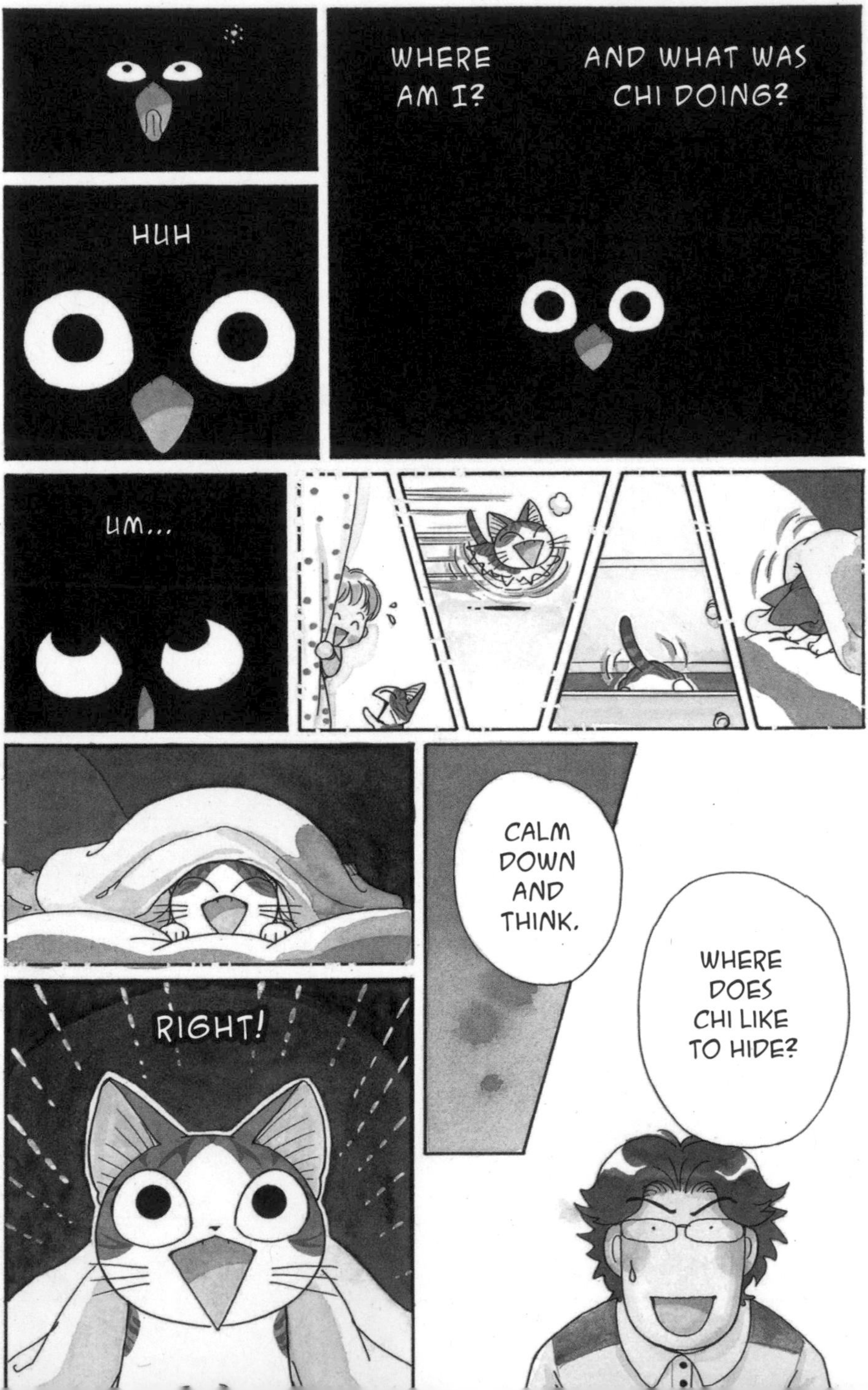
WHERE AM I?
AND WHAT WAS CHI DOING?
HUH
UM...
RIGHT!
CALM DOWN AND THINK.
WHERE DOES CHI LIKE TO HIDE?

CHI LIKES TO HIDE IN BAGS.
RIGHT.
SHE LIKES BASKETS AND BOXES TOO.
BOXES AND BAGS!
TIME TO LOOK!
I'LL LOOK UP-STAIRS.
THUD
THUD
THUD
KLAK
BLOCK
THUNK
THAT MEANS...
HE HASN'T FOUND ME YET.
MEOW
YEAH! CHI WON!
HEY?

WHAT HAPPENED?
NOT HERE?
HMM?
SHE LIKES TO HIDE BEHIND THINGS TOO.
SHE DIVES INTO LAUNDRY.
AND UNDER BLANKETS AND BEHIND DOORS.
IN SHADOWS, EH...
THAT'S RIGHT.
SHUV SHUV

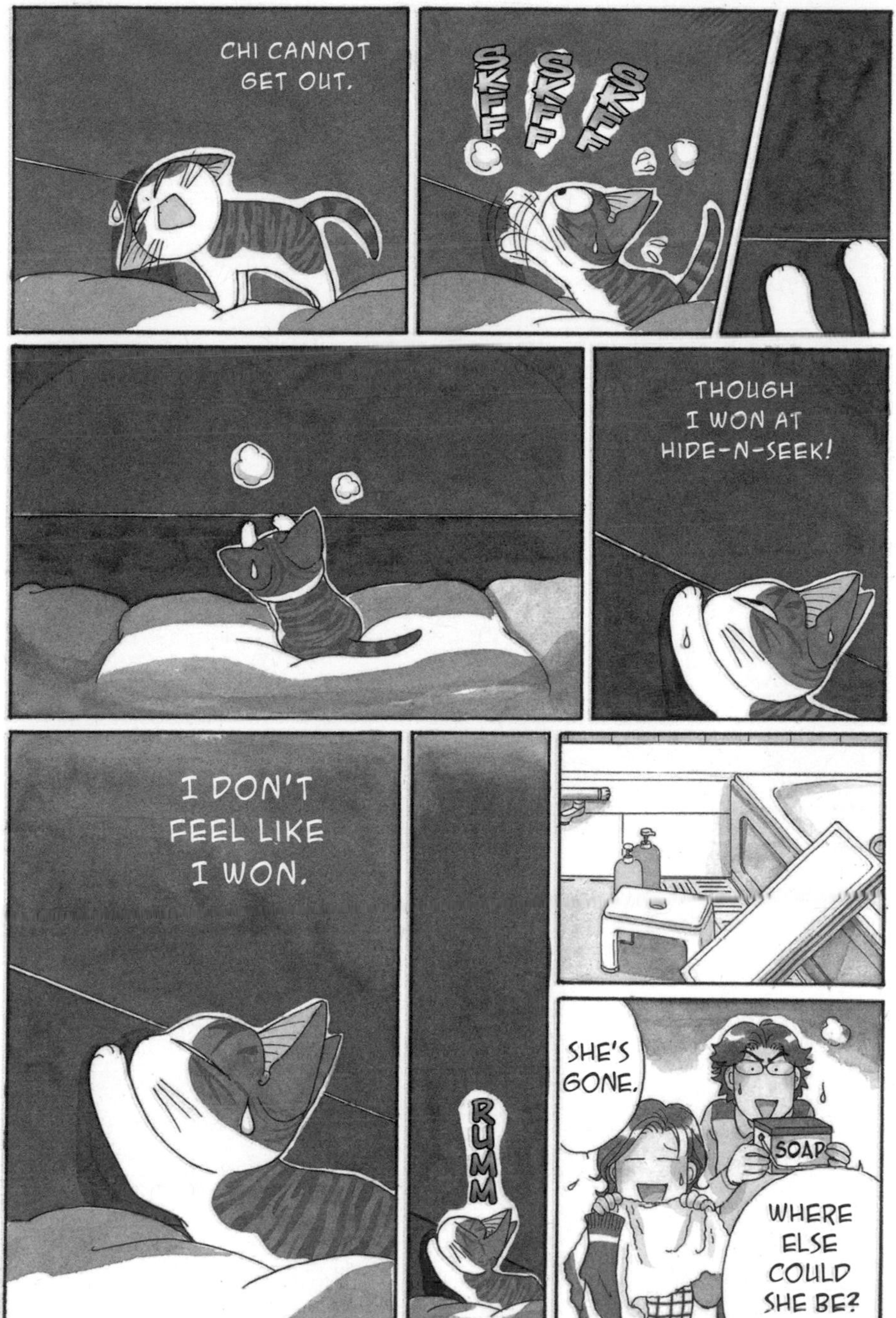
CHI CANNOT GET OUT.
SKFF
SKFF
SKFF
THOUGH I WON AT HIDE-N-SEEK!
I DON'T FEEL LIKE I WON.
RUMM
SHE'S GONE.
SOAP
WHERE ELSE COULD SHE BE?

CHI LOVES TO HIDE BACK HERE!
CREVICES!
SHE'S SLID INTO REALLY NARROW SPACES BEFORE.
LIKE THE MOVING BOXES...
YEAH, EVEN THIS NARROW.
RIGHT.
CHI!
RUMBL
RRUMBL
CHI'S HUNGRY!
NOT HERE.
WHERE ELSE COULD CHI HAVE GONE?
I HOPE NOTHING HAS HAPPENED.
IN SHADOWS
BOXES AND
AND REALLY NARROW SPOTS.
THIS NARROW!

NO WAY ...
HUH ?
GRROWL
GRRRUMBL
CHI WANTS TO LOSE!
SKFF SKFF SKFF
MYA MYA
LEMME OUT! LEMME OUT!
MYA MYA MYA
SKF SKF SKF
SKFF SKFF SKFF
MYA
CHI WANTS TO LOSE!
WHAM

SHE'S HERE!
MIYA
YOU FOUND ME!
CHI'S PRETTY GOOD AT HIDE-N-SEEK, HUH?
YUP
YAY! CHI LOST!
MEOW

the end

homemade 74: a cat chases

SNIF
SNIF SNIF SNIF
CHI KNOWS THIS SMELL.
WHAT IS IT?
I WONDER.
HAH
DAD, WE BOUGHT YOU A PRESENT.
YOHEI, WASH YOUR HANDS FIRST, OKAY.
OH!
RUSTLE RUSTLE

WHAT A GOOD SMELL.
WOW!
MIYA
TIME TO DIG IN!
PUF PUF
HA!
!
THIS IS HOT!
SO HOT!

OH, RIGHT!
NEED TO DO THIS.
SWEF SWEF SWEF
OH
HEY, CHI!
MEOW
EEK!
GOTTA RUN!
ESCAPE!
BOUND

RUN!
DASH—
CLIMB! CLIMB!
BOING
BOING
THEY GOT MAD AT ME AGAIN.
AH?
AGAIN?
WHAT HAPPENED "AGAIN"?
CHI

SAY,
YOU CAN HAVE ONE.
MYA
OH!
WHY DID I CLIMB SO HIGH?
WHY?

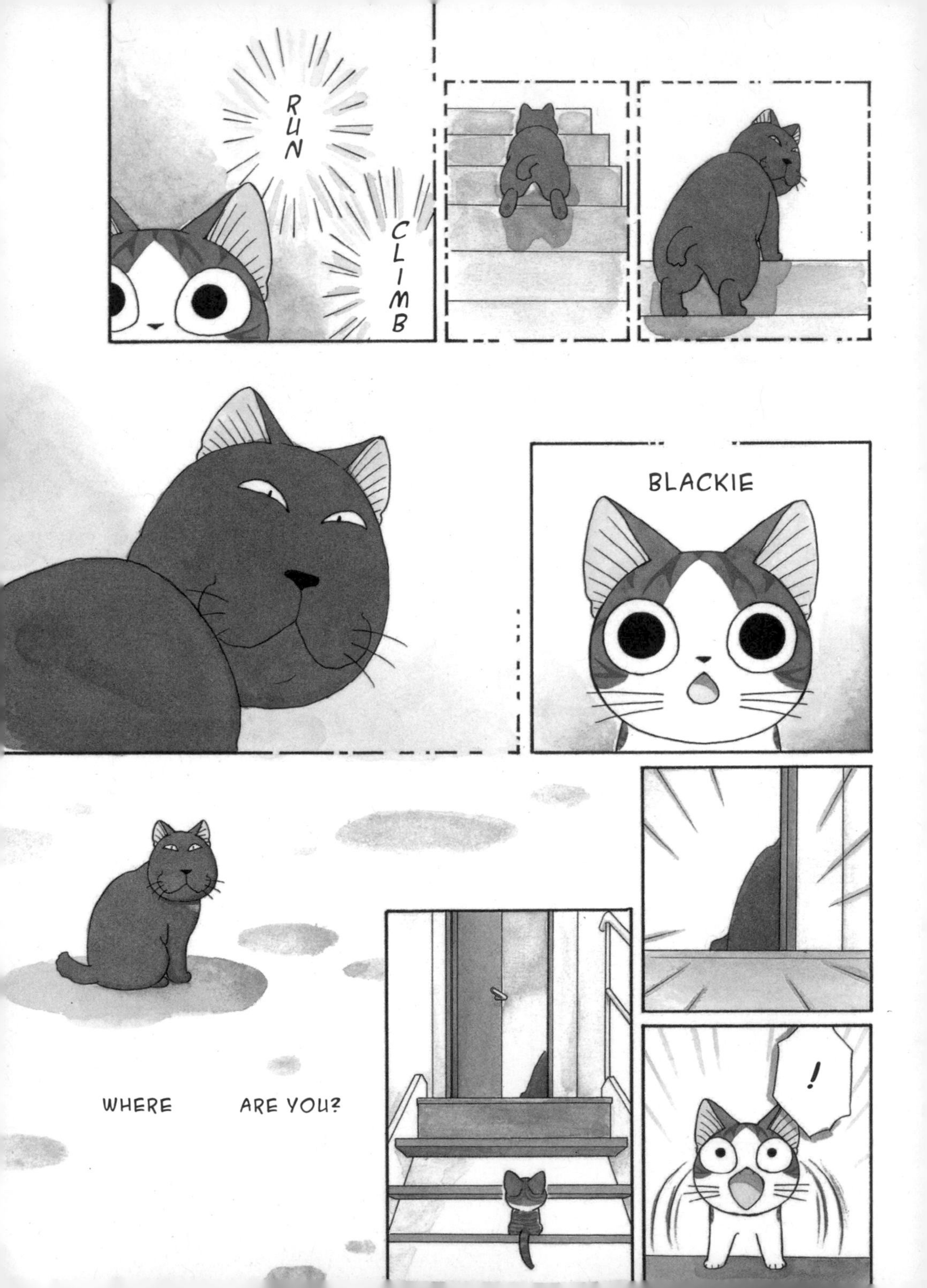
RUN
CLIMB
BLACKIE
WHERE
ARE YOU?
!

BLACKIE
BOING BOING
BOING
MYA MYA
HEY! HEY!
...

COME, CHI.
CHI!
THUP
THUP
HOW TROUBLE-SOME.
WE'VE GOT FRIED CHICKEN FOR YOU TOO.
...

the end

homemade 75: a cat welcomes

SWISH
WHAT'S UP?
TMP
WHAT THE?
?!

HOW DO YOU DO?
NYA
HUH?
NYA
I BELIEVE WE MET LAST WEEK.
FLUF
RIGHT!
NYA
HUH, SO YOU LIVE HERE?

MYA
WHY'D YOU COME BY?
MIYA
YOU WANNA PLAY WITH CHI?
HEY, HEY~
MIYA MIYA
SWISH
HUH?
NO PLAYING?
MIYA
MIYA
LET'S PLAY.
MIYA
COME ON, LET'S PLAY!
SNIFF
SNIFF
SNIFF
SNIFF
WANNA PLAY?
MIYA
SKIP
SKIP
SKIP
SKIP
SKIP
SKIP
MIYA
LET'S PLAY!
HALT

OH?
SWISH
MYA
LET'S PLAY!
PEE PEE PEE
GWAR
MYA
WOW
YAY
MEOW
MY,
THE NEIGHBOR'S CAT.
OH?
DASH

WOAH
WHAT A PRETTY GUEST.
IT'S ALICE.
ALICE?
RIGHT. SHE LIVES ON THE FIRST FLOOR.
HOW PRETTY.
SHE'S LIKE A DOLL.
HI!
OUT FOR A WALK?
DASH
PANT PANT PANT
MIYA
WE WERE PLAYING!
TILT
WOW
OH!
MY
HOW ABOUT A SNACK?

THERE YOU GO.
YAY
MIYA
LET'S EAT!
MIYA
MUNCH
MUNCH
SNFF SNFF
AH?
IT'S TASTY.
MEOW
WHAT'S WRONG?
FWIP
SWISH
?
MAYBE SHE ONLY EATS THOSE?
DE-LUXE CAT CHOW?
POSSIBLY.

SHE'S ELE-GANT,
AND HAS CLASS.
CHI AND ALICE ARE COMPLETE OPPOSITES.
MEOW
CHI'S STUFFED !
I CAN'T BELIEVE THEY'RE BOTH CATS.
AND CHI ATE BOTH DISHES.
THROW OUT THE PAPER, YOHEI.
OKAY
KSH
KSH
PLUNK
KSH
KSH
KSH

MIW
RISE
WHOA!
KSH
OH?
MEOW
YEAH
DART
SKOOT SKOOT
SKOOT
SKOOT
SKOOT
NYA
MYA
DASH—
NYA
WOO HOO!
DASH
SKAT
THEY'RE CLEARLY BOTH CATS.
YUP.

the end

homemade 76: a cat sleeps

PFF
PFF
PFF
WHERE SHOULD I SLEEP?
PFF
PFF
PFF
AH!
PFF
PFF
PFF

SO FWUFFY.
AND SO COZY.
SIDLE
DADDY'S SMELL.
MIYA
WHAT A NICE SPOT.
NITE NITE ...
M
MMPH...
MMPH...

BWAH!
FLOP
WHAT?
...
OH!
A CAVE!
SHFF
SHFF
SHFF
MEOW
ANOTHER NICE SPOT.

GOOD NIGHT.
WHUM
MEOW?!
...
CHI'S GONNA SLEEP IN A NICER SPOT.
TAP
TAP
TAP
TAP

OH!
A HIGH PLACE!
SRWW
SRWW
SRWW
MEOW
HOW ABOUT THAT! TEE-HEE!
G'NIGHT!
THUD

...
SLIP—
THUMP
GRRR
STIFF
...
...
STUFF
STUFF
...

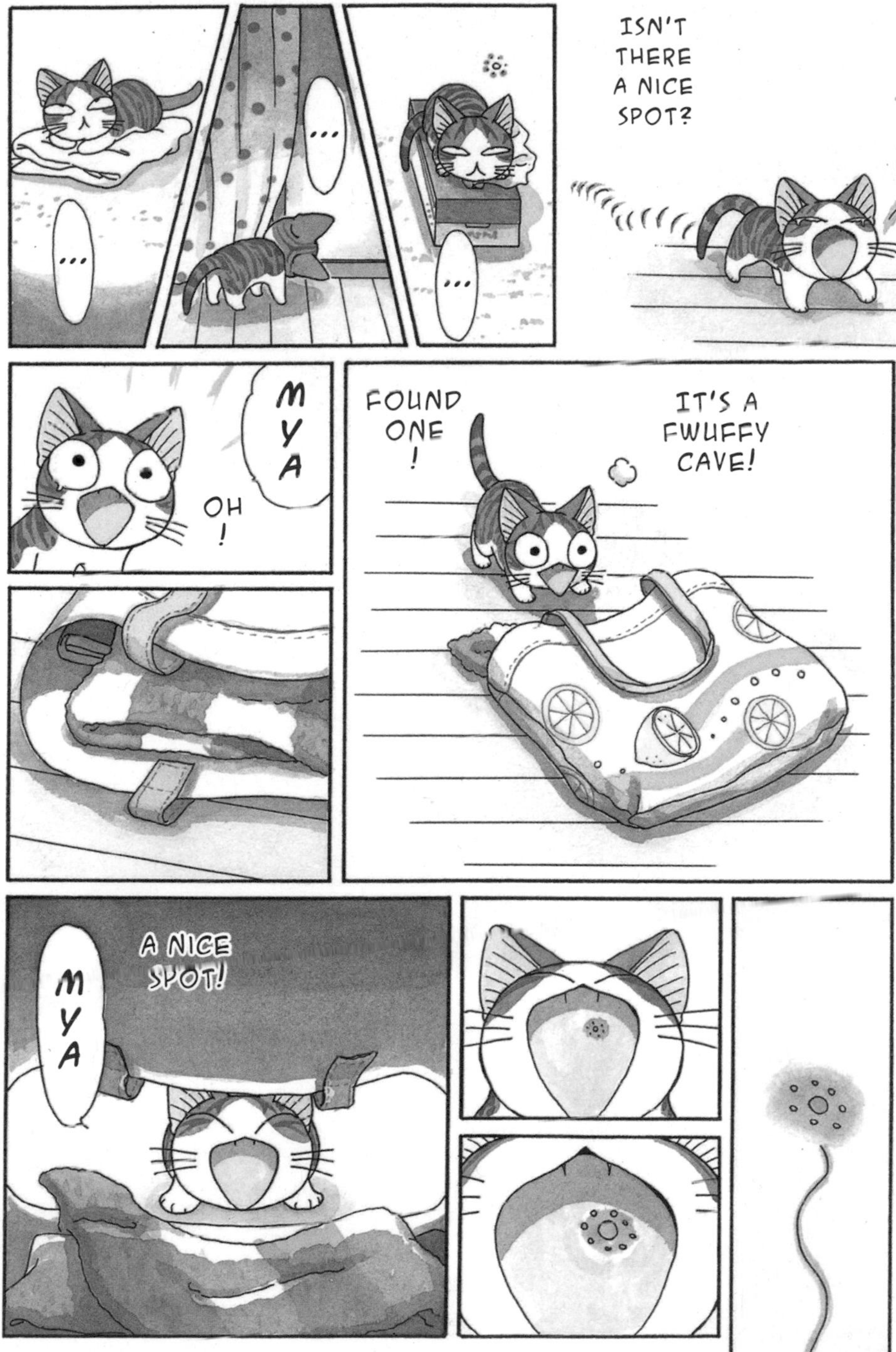
...
...
...
ISN'T THERE A NICE SPOT?
YAWN
MYA
OH!
FOUND ONE!
IT'S A FWUFFY CAVE!
MYA
A NICE SPOT!

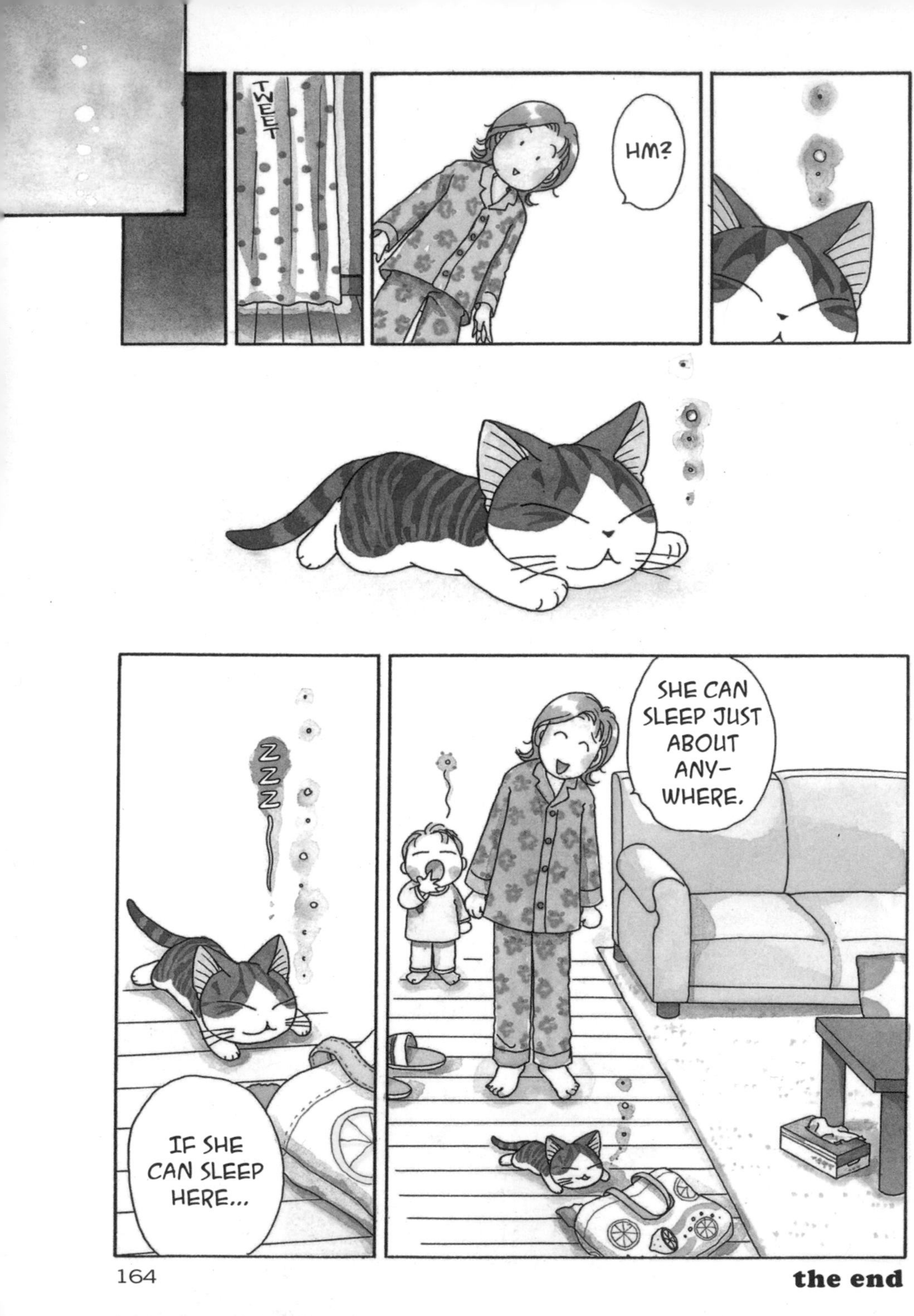
TWEET
HM?
ZZZ
SHE CAN SLEEP JUST ABOUT ANY-WHERE.
IF SHE CAN SLEEP HERE...

the end

homemade 77: a cat investigates

BZZZ
BZZZ
BZZZ
BZZZ
BZZZ
BZZZ
MIYA MIYA
WHAT KINDA NOISE IS THAT?
BZZZ
EMPTY~
NO ONE'S HERE.
BZZZ

BNNN—
BNNN—
BNNN—
WHAT IS IT?
WHAT?
KSSH
KSSH
KSSH
BNNN—
BNNN—
BNNN—
NNNN
NNNN
OVER THERE!
BNNN—
BNNN—
SKEE
SKEE
BZ...
...
DOINK
HUH?
I WAS SURE IT WAS HERE...
MEMO
WNCH

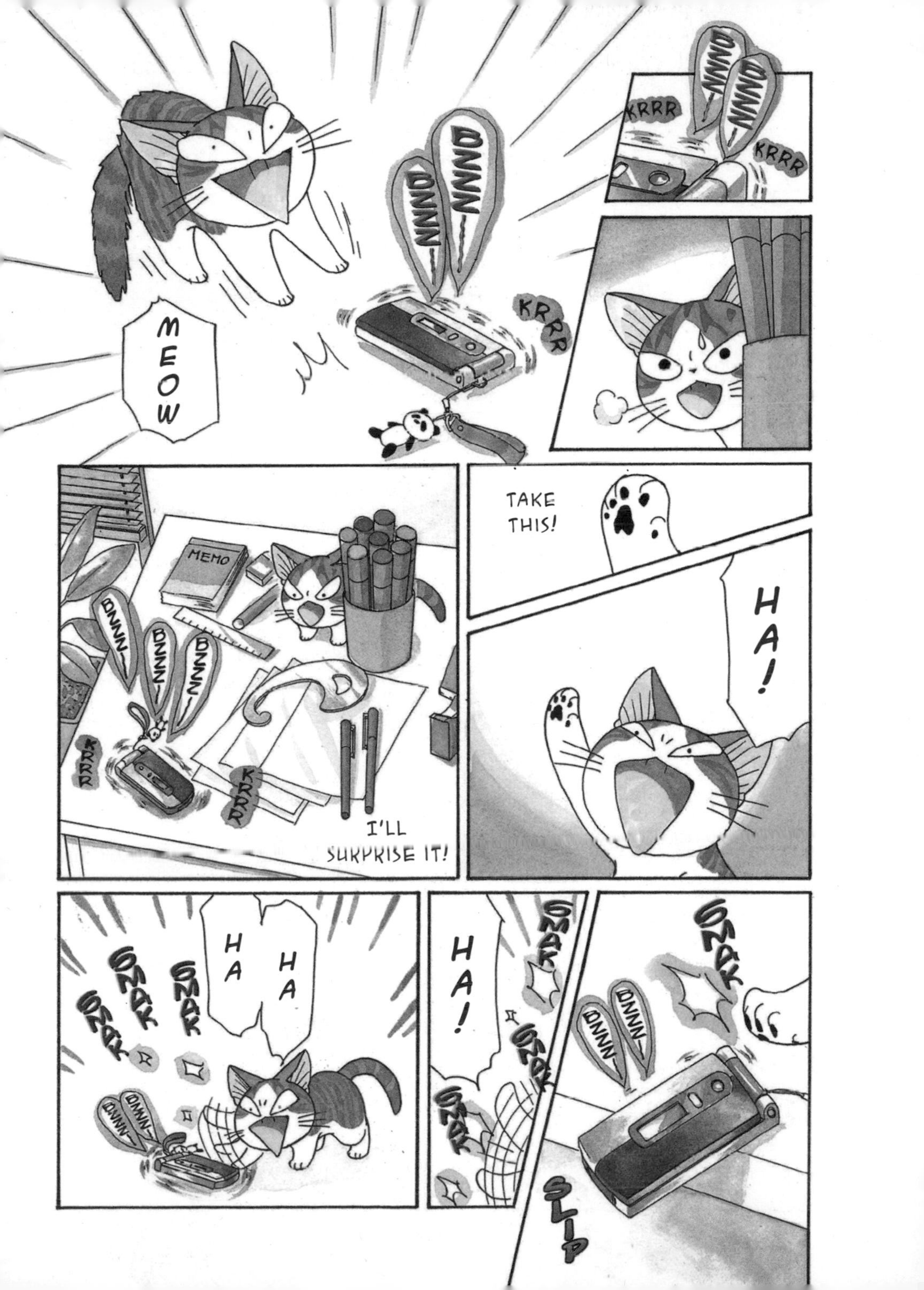
KRRR
BZZZ
KRRR
BZZZ
KRRR
MEOW
TAKE THIS!
I'LL SURPRISE IT!
BZZZ
KRRR
KRRR
HA!
SMAK
SLIP
HA!
SMAK
SMAK
HA HA
SMAK
SMAK
SMAK

WOOSH!!
BZZ
BZZ
TUNK
PLOP
BZZ
BZZ
BZZ
TICK
HEH
MEOW
CHI DID IT!
OH...

IT'S THE FIRST TIME I'VE BEEN IN THIS ROOM.
TIME TO INVESTI-GATE.
SNIFF
SNIFF
SNIFF
SNIFF
SNIFF
SNIFF
SNIFF
SNIFF
SNIFF
SNIFF
THIS ALL SEEMS TO BE
DADDY'S TURF.
...
GRIN

MYA
IT'S CHI'S, TOO!
RUB RUB RUB
THIS TOO.
SKFF SKFF SKFF
CHI'S STUFF!
T-W-I-N-G-E
HERE!
AND OVER HERE TOO!
ROLL ROLL ROLL...
ROLL ROLL
ROLL ROLL
ROLL
ROLL
HA
IT'S ALL CHI'S STUFF!
MIYA
HUH?

AH?
MYA?!
STICK
SHAKE SHAKE
SHAKE SHAKE
HEY?
?!
TAP TAP TAP...
!
EEK
FLOP
TURN
DASH...
HUFF
HUFF
HUFF
FWIP

!!
MEOW
HEWLP ME!!
MEOW MEOW
SOME-ONE HELP!
OH...
...
NO ONE'S HOME.

the end

homemade 78: a cat feigns ignorance

WHAT SHOULD I DO?
GWAR
WARR

DON'T FOLLOW ME!
HA!
LET GO! LEMME GO!
HA!
SWIP
SWIP
SWIP
SWIP
STICK
!
MEOW
NO, NO, NO!
WHIP WHIP WHIP
WHIP WHIP
WHIP WHIP
TWANG
PEEL

PHEW.
SHFF SHFF
BUT,
SOMETHING FUNNY IS GOING ON.
SHFF SHFF
TAP TAP TAP
SHFF SHFF
WHAT SHOULD I DO?
WANDER
WANDER
WANDER
!
IT'S GOTTEN EVEN FUNNIER!
SHFF
SHFF
SHFF SHFF
TAP TAP TAP TAP
SHFF
EEEK!
TAP TAP TAP TAP—
EEEEP!
SHFF SHFF—

DASH—
MIYA
YIKES
SHFF—
KLATTER
TWANG
PEEL
PLOP
IT'S OFF!
MEOW
OH?

KLAM
KLAK
NGA?!
THUD
WHAM
BAM
BAM
WHUM
BONK
SNAP
ROLL ROLL
CRACK
ROLL...
WHAT THE...

THEY'RE GONNA BE MAD!
...
WHAT NOW?
TIP
SCRITCH SCRITCH
GRIN
I'LL JUST PLAY DUMB!
MYA
HOP
!

THE STEP-STEPS!
YIKES
BUT I CAN'T GO BACK.
HOP
RUN!
SKIP SKIP
RUN!
SKIP SKIP
I'M OUTTA HERE!
HUFF HUFF HUFF
HA

SNICKER
CHI DOESN'T KNOW A THING.
CHI
WE'RE BACK!
WOAH!
THE SECOND FLOOR IS A MESS!
THIS WAS CHI'S WORK.
THERE'S FUR ON THE TAPE ...
IT WASN'T CHI.

the end

homemade 79: a cat contrives

WHAP WHAP
YAY YAY
TAP TAP
HEE HEE
REZZY REZZY
MYA?
WHAT'S THIS NOW?
MIYA
CHI'S GOING TOO.
SKTT SKTT SKTT SKTT
MYA
OPEN UP.
SKTT SKTT SKTT
SKTT SKTT SKTT
OPEN!
MYA

SKTT SKTT
OPEN THIS UP!
MYA
HUH?
OH
AH, CHI ...
I CAN SEE FROM HERE.
MIYA
I CAN SEE.

SHUV
MYA?!
SO YOU'VE FOUND THE CAT DOOR.
SHUV
C'MON, CHI,
TRY GOING THROUGH IT.
SHUV SHUV
MEOW
WHATCHA DOING?
GRIP
SHUV SHUV
MEOW
WHAT?
GRIP
GAPE
CHOMP
OH BOY, WHAT'S IN THAT HEAD?
GRR GRR
AAAAA
TEE HEE
WHY CAN'T SHE FIGURE IT OUT?
HURTS

HEY?
FLAP
MEE
HUH?
FLA
THAP
MYA
WHAT ARE THEY DOING?
MIYAH
ARGH
FLOP
BONK
WHAT?
HUP
FLAP
WHAT WAS THAT FOR?
MEOW
HOP

IT WAS KLIK-KLAKING BEFORE TOO!
HA
TRY THAT AGAIN!!
SWID
SWID
SWID
KRIK
KRIK
KRIK
TIK
NO COUNTER-ATTACK.
...
PUSH

OPEN
CLOSE
OPEN
CLOSE
WHAT IS THIS ?
I'VE GOTTA THINK.
THINK
THINK
?!
OH!

TILT
NUDGE
PUSH
TAP TAP TAP
MIYA
CHI MADE A BIG DISCOVERY!

OH!
WOW!
CHI'S USING THE CAT DOOR!
STRUT
STRUT
STRUT
YOU'VE FIGURED IT OUT, CHI.
GOOD GOOD
HEH HEH
MIYA
CHI USED HER HEAD!
BOP
IF I USE MY HEAD, IT OPENS!
MEOW

the end

homemade 80: a cat is brushed

SKRCH
SKRCH
SKRCH
SKRCH
SKRCH
SKRCH
SKRCH
SKRCH
SKRCH
SKRCH
WE HAVEN'T BRUSHED HER YET, HAVE WE?

LICK
LICK
LICK
CHI
LOOK, IT'S A BRUSH FOR CHI.
LET ME BRUSH YOU.
WHAT'S THAT?
?
FWIP
LICK
LICK
LICK
LICK
PAD

WHAT ARE YOU UP TO, DADDY?
MEOW
SEE?
BRUSH
BRUSH
BRUSH
BRUSH
BRUSH
BRUSH
WHOA?!
PAT
MYA?

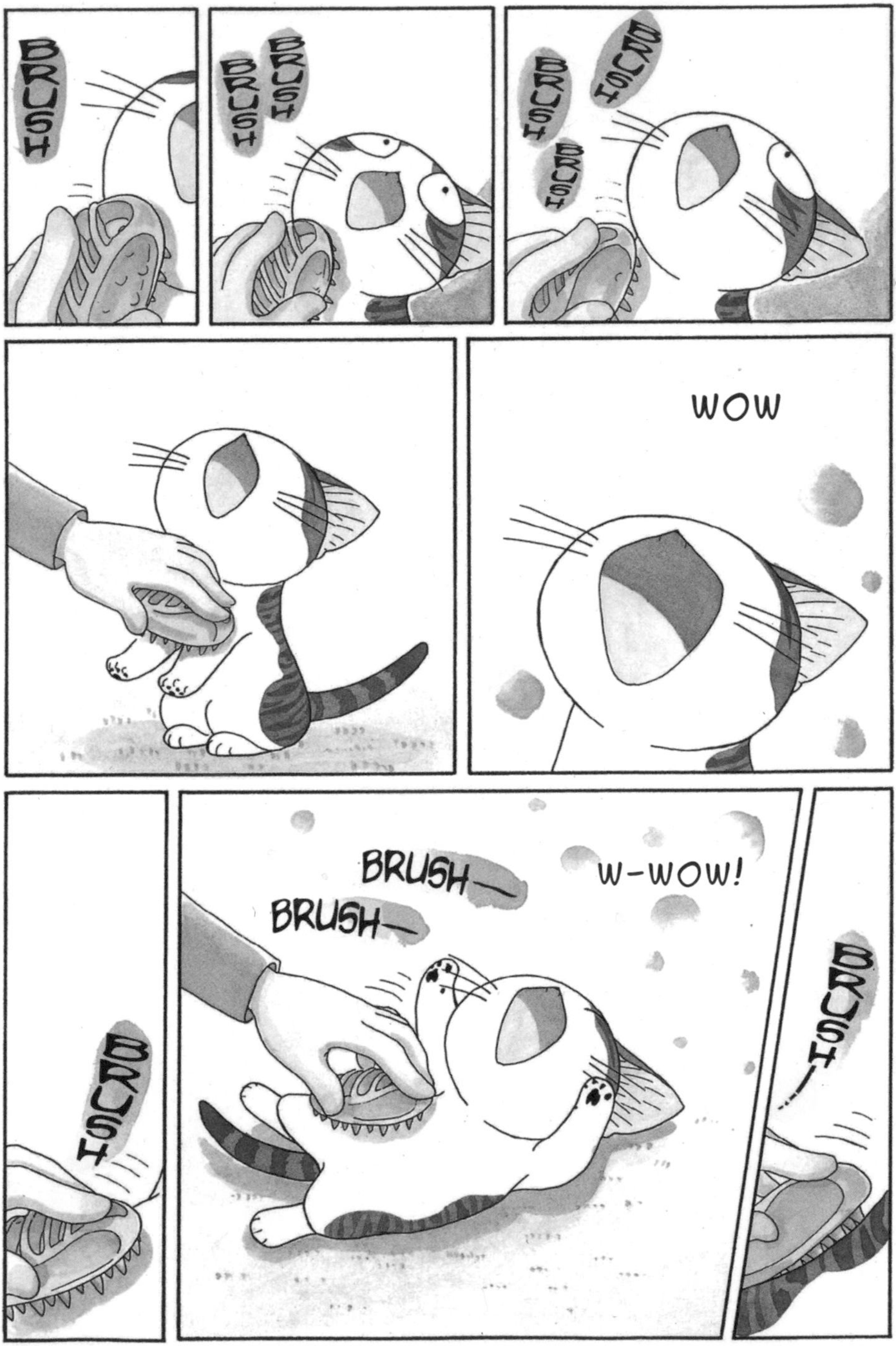
BRUSH
BRUSH
BRUSH
BRUSH
BRUSH
BRUSH
WOW
BRUSH
BRUSH—
BRUSH—
W-WOW!
BRUSH—

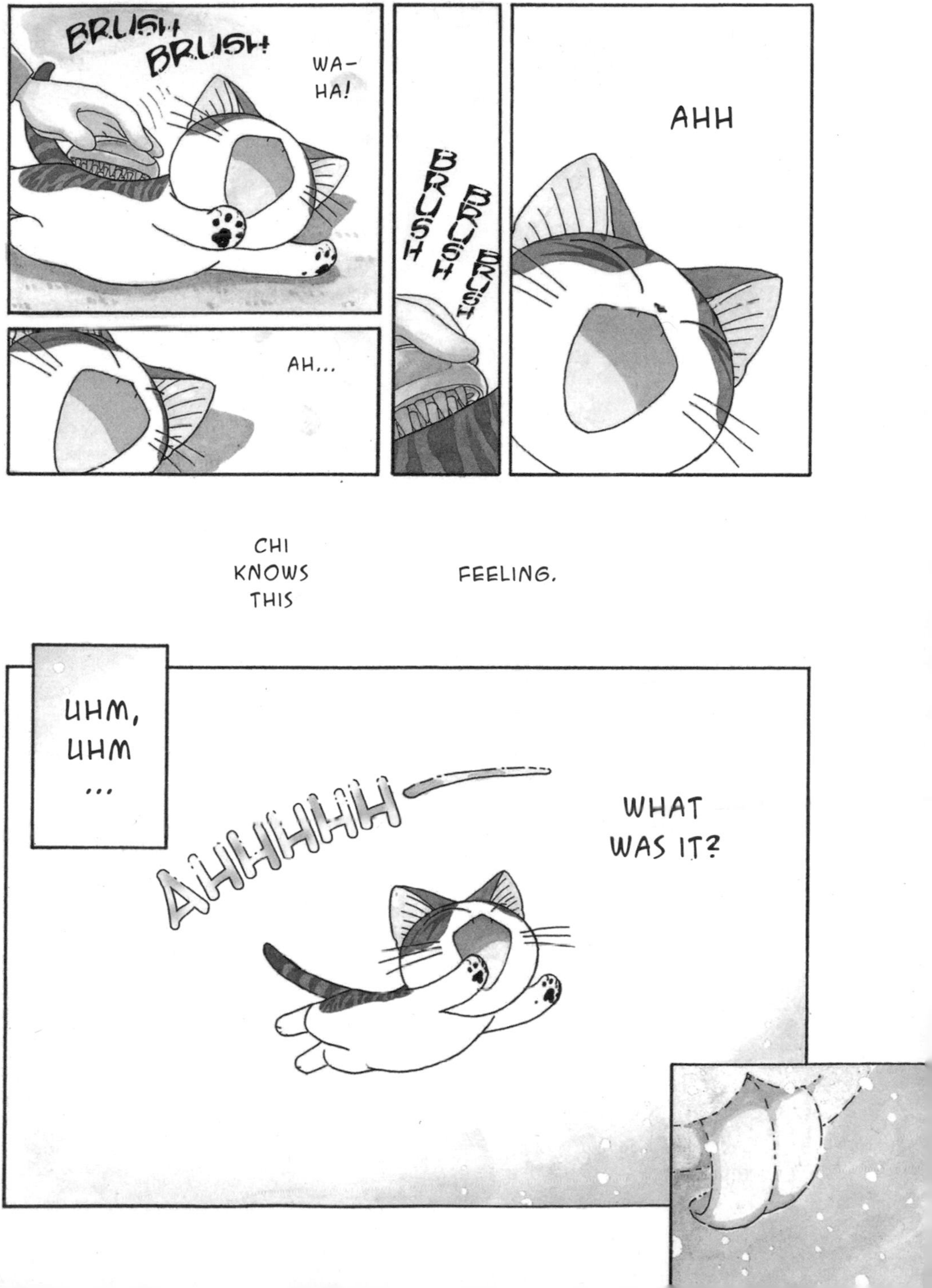
BRUSH BRUSH
WA-HA!
AH...
BRUSH BRUSH BRUSH
AHH
CHI KNOWS THIS FEELING.
UHM, UHM ...
AHHHHHH
WHAT WAS IT?

HMM

HEY?
WOAH
HA HA!
A LITTLE BLANKET.
PLIK PLIK PLIK
PLIK

I GUESS WE SHOULD BRUSH HER NOW AND THEN.
RIGHT, CHI?
MOM
MOM
YOU KNOW WHAT?
CHI ...
IS BEING REALLY FUNNY!

TIP TIP TIP
TIP TIP TIP TIP
SHE'S FOLLOWING DAD AROUND EVERY-WHERE.
I WONDER WHAT'S GOTTEN INTO HER?
ALL I DID WAS BRUSH HER.
NUZZL

the end

homemade 81: a cat goes out

LET'S GO, DAVID!
WOOF
RRUFF WUF
MYA!
THAT VOICE!
ZSHK
ZSHK
ZASH

WOOF
IT'S BARKS FROM NEXT DOOR... I KNEW IT!
MIYA
MIYA
WOOF WOOF
WHERE ARE YOU GOING?
OH?
PANT
PANT
PANT
HE'S GONE.
HEY?
VROOM

WOW!
MIYA
WHERE AM I?
TIP TIP TIP
MIYA
HUH?
MYA
WHAT IS THIS?
SMAK SMAK SMAK
MYA
WHAZZAT?
MIYA
WHAT'S WITH THIS HOLE?
MYA
SO TINY!

MYA
WHERE YA GOING?
MYA?
HUH?
WHAT'S THIS?
IT'S HUGE!

SO FAR...
BO-ING
BO-ING
HOW FAR DOES IT GO?

WHERE DOES IT...
GO?
...
PANT
PANT
RUFF
MYA
THEY'RE BACK!
MEOW
HEY, HEY, HEY!
HOW FAR DOES IT GO?
MEOW

OH
WOOF
RUFF
RUFF
WOOF
...
CHI
CHI
SHAK
CHI
YESH
MIYA
SKOOT!!...
HALT

IT GOES ON
IT STARTS HERE.
OUTSIDE CHI'S YARD.
MYA
I'M HOME!

the end

homemade 82: a cat is thrilled

SKAT!...
MYA
CHI'S GONNA TAKE OFF, TOO!

THAT WAY.
MIYA
I'LL GO SEE.
TIP
TIP
TIP
SHOOP
HM?
I DON'T KNOW THAT ONE.
SAUNTER
SAUNTER
WHERE'S SHE GOING?
WHAT'S OVER THERE?

GRIN
TAP TAP TAP
TIP TIP TIP TIP
WHERE YA GOING?
TIP TIP TIP
HEY?
BISTRO
Park Side
WHAT'S HERE?
SNAP
HEY!
DASH—

TIP TIP TIP
TAP TAP TAP
WHAT SORTA PWACE ARE WE GOING?
TIP TIP TIP
OH?
KOSH KOSH
KOSH KOSH KOSH
MIYA
THAT'S ALL KRINCKLY!
KOSH KOSH KOSH
TIP TIP TIP
SNAP
MEOW
KYA!
BACK ON TRACK, CHI!
DASH

TAP
TAP
TAP
TAP
WOW!
CHI'LL WALK HERE, TOO.
TID
TID
TID
TID
TID
TID
TID
WHAT NOW?
FLIP
BOUND
AHH!

CHI'S GOING TOO!
CROUCH
CROUCH
CROUCH
SPROING
MEOW
SNAR
CRIK
CRIK
CRIK
CRIK
SKRRRK
SIGH

I CAN'T JUMP THAT HIGH.
CHI
CAN'T GO ON.
TIP TIP TIP
HN?
TIP TIP TIP
DOH

GO ON, GO ON!
WHAT'S NEXT ?
DASH
WOW !

the end

homemade 83: a cat explores

WHOA!
MYA
LOOKS LIKE FUN!
DASH—

RUFF
HUFF
DART
HUFF
WOOF
WOOF
HUFF
MEOW
NOT A BARKS!
GAG
KYAN
KYAN
KYAN
YANK
HUH?
AH HA...
BLEH!

HEH HEH
CHI WINS!
AHEM, AHEM!
TIP TIP TIP
SHOOP
KYA
MYA
OOH!
SHOOP
WHAT'S THAT?
MIYA
SKOOT

SHOOP
MEOW
ROLL
SHUMP
HOP
HUFF
MIYA
SOME-THING STWANGE UP THERE.
SHOOP
YAY
MIYA

MEOW
SCAREWY FUN!
DASH
THMP
SWAY SWAY
AHH!
MEOW
IT'S SWING-ING!
MYA
WAIT UP!
HOP HOP HOP
MYA
WAIT!
HOP HOP HOP
MEOW
SO MUCH FUN!

MIYA
HOP HOP HOP
WHAT'S NEXT?
MIYA
OH!
MYA
SO MUCH SAND!
MYA
MIYA
MIYA
DASH
MEOW
SO MANY FUN THINGS!

HM?

...?
MYA?!
SPLISH
MEOW
WHAZZAT?!
DASH——...

the end

homemade 84: a cat returns

PLIP
PLIP
MYA
WHEE!
SPLISSH
PLIP
PLIP
SKOOT—...
MEOW
WHAT'S THIS WAY?
PARK PLAZA #1
ANNEX

WOW!
WANDER
WANDER
WANDER
MEOW
SO MANY TWEES.
WOOSH
HUH?
HMM?
MYA
CHI KNOWS THIS PLACE!

MIYA
DASHI
I KNOW! I KNOW!
MEOW
IT'S HOME!
DASH—
SHK SHK
SWAK
CHI'S HOME ...
IT'S HOME,
BUT IT'S NOT CHI'S.
SHK SHK SHK

TIP TIP TIP TIP
WHERE HAVE I SEEN HER BEFORE ...
NYA
MUMBLE MUMBLE
TIP TIP
NYA
SAY, YOU ...
HMM?
NIYA
WHERE ARE YOU FROM, LITTLE ONE?
I'M NOT LITTLE ONE!
MYAH
I'M CHI.
I'M CHI...
MEOW
OF CHI'S HOME!

FWP
TAP TAP TAP TAP TAP
MYA
CHI'S GOING HOME!
HRM?
TURN
TAP TAP TAP TAP
CHI KNOWS THIS PLACE TOO!

TAP TAP TAP TAP
CHI'S GOING HOME.
THAT'S NOT CHI'S HOME.
TAP TAP TAP TAP
FSSH
FSSH
FSSH
UHM
ERR

HMMM
HM-M-M
NIYA
SAY, LITTLE ONE...
NYA
WHOSE LITTLE ONE WERE YOU, NOW?
CHI...
MYA...
WHAT'S THE MATTER, LITTLE ONE?
NYAH?

MEOWR?!
WHOSE LITTLE ONE IS CHI, PWEEZ?!
SAY WHAT ?!
GRROWL
NYA
WHY DON'T YOU COME WITH ME?
...
RMBL
PLOD PLOD

the end

homemade 85: a cat is invited

MUNCH
KRUNCH
MUNCH
KRUNCH
MYA
WHERE IS CHI'S HOME?
HMMM ...
NIEE

HMM ...
NYA
PLEASE REMEMBER.
MYA
I'VE SEEN YOU BEFORE ...
NYA
LITTLE ONE?
NYA
IT'S CHI!
MYA
...
HOW ABOUT JOINING US HERE?
NIYA
WHA-

NYA
IT'S SPACIOUS...
AND LAID BACK.
NIU
BUT USE THAT CUSHION OVER THERE.
NYA
...
THIS ONE'S MY FAVORITE, SO NO TOUCHING.
NIYA
BUT...
MYA
PUT YOUR SCENT ON IT AND IT'S YOURS.
NYA

RUB RUB
RUB RUB
SNFF SNFF SNFF SNFF
IT'S GOT CHI'S SMELL, SO NOW IT'S CHI'S.
SNFF...
NIYA
A FINE FLUFFY-WUFFY CUSHION, ISN'T IT?
NYA
WHAT DO YOU SAY?

MIU
SOME-THING'S NOT RIGHT.
IT'S GOT CHI'S SMELL...
NYA
WHAT ISN'T?
BUT SOMETHING'S NOT RIGHT.
MEOW
CHI'S GOING HOME!
NIYA
SO YOU KNOW YOUR WAY BACK?

FIP
...
I WANNA GO HOME!
MEOWR
WUF WUF
HN?

RUFF
MYA
MYA
IT'S BARKS FROM NEXT DOOR.
CHI'S GOING HOME NOW!
MYA
SPRING
MIYA
BYE-BYE!
WUF
WUF
MY, MY...
OH!
THAT'S IT!

ROLL ROLL
ROLL ROLL
HOME! HOME!
MYA
CHI'S SMELL!
YOHEY'S SMELL,
SNFF
AND DADDY'S SMELL,
AND MOMMY'S SMELL.
CHI GOT TO SPEND THE WHOLE DAY OUTSIDE.
ALL HAPPY, EH?
MIYA
I REMEMBER THAT LITTLE ONE NOW...

the end

homemade 86: a cat doesn't mesh

CHI, LETS PLAY!
MIYA
LET'S PLAY!
PLUNK

OKAY
PLUNK
PLUNK
PLUNK
PLUNK
MYA?
WHAT?
CHI, LET'S BUILD A BASE!
PRETTY COOL, HUH?
?
TIP TIP TIP...

HEY?
TIP TIP TIP...
DRAT
FLOP
FLOP
WHAT CAN YOU DO...
MIYA
POUNCE
YANK
YANK
GNAW GNAW
MEOW
SAY, THIS IS PRETTY FUN.
MEOW
LET'S PLAY, YOHEY!
HMM?

ALOK
HEY?
MYA
BUT THIS IS SO MUCH FUN.
OH?
WOAH!
MIYA
YOHEY, LOOK, I FOUND SOMETHING AMAZING.
CHI, COME CHECK THIS OUT!

...
...
MYA
KLOP
KLOP
OOPS!
OH MY ...

YOU TWO MADE QUITE A MESS.
MAKE SURE TO CLEAN UP, OKAY.
OK
MYA?
KLUNK
KLUNK
OH
FWOM
MYA?
WOW
DON'T GO IN THERE, CHI.
I'M GOING IN.
MEOW

CHI, STOP!
MYA
PUSH PUSH
CHI
ROLL...
MYA
FLICK

ROLL...
I WONDER IF THEY'RE DONE.
TOSS
FLICK
MEOW
ROLL.....

the end

homemade 87: a cat does mesh

ALL PACKED UP?
TURN
AH!
MYA?
PLAYING TOGETHER, I SEE.

MEOW
DON'T CLIMB IN, CHI.
LOOKS LIKE YOU'RE STILL COPYING EACH OTHER.
GIGGLE
CLEAN UP AND WE'LL HAVE SNACKS.
SKOT
YAY!
SKOT
WAIT UP!
MIYA
WAIT FOR ME!
MEOW
SNACK TIME!
WOW!
MYA?
THANKS FOR THE TREAT!
MEOW
WHAT IS THIS?
STILL AT IT, HUH?
CHI, YOU'RE A CAT, SO YOURS IS HERE.
TUNK
SEE?

LAP LAP LAP
TUP
MYA?
WHAT'S THIS?
STARE
WHAT'S UP, CHI?
DID I DROP THAT?
MYA?
OH MY.
A PAIR OF COPY-CATS.

HM?
SO CHI AND YOHEI WERE MIMICKING EACH OTHER?
A CAT AND A HUMAN?
I KNOW.
WELCOME BACK, DAD!
HI,
AND CHI?
LOAF
MYA?
HAH HAH!
READ ME THIS!
STRETCH

RIP
HEY, STOP THAT.
RIP
RIP
RIP
PLUNK
YOOOOH
COME HERE, CHI!
POOF
POOF
POOF
RUB
RUB
RUB

MUFF MUFF
SNATCH
MEOW
IF YOU LET IT DANGLE, CHI'S GONNA TAKE A RIDE.
WANNA PLAY?
MIYA
CHI, PLEASE STOP.
GRSH GRSH
MEOW MEOW
MEOW
THIS IS FUN.
CHI'S A CAT...

MEOW MEOW
THIS ISN'T FOR PLAYING.
BAH!
MYA
THEY DO THE SAME THINGS FOR OTHER REASONS.
MYA MYA KYA
YUP.
M....
HUSH
HMM?
WHY SO QUIET...
WHAT HAPPENED?!

ASLEEP?
JUST LIKE THAT?
SOUND ASLEEP
AH, SUDDENLY FALLING ASLEEP...
CLEARLY, THEY'RE BOTH "CHILDREN."
AND SYNCHED, AT THAT.

the end

homemade 88: a cat halts

WHOA
WHAT NICE WEATHER.

KPAK
MIYA
CHI WILL BE BACK SOON.
I'LL GO THAT WAY TODAY.
I WONDER WHAT'S DOWN THERE.
MYA
CHI'LL KEEP GOING STRAIGHT.
GO!
MEOW
TIP TIP TIP
FIP FIP
TURN

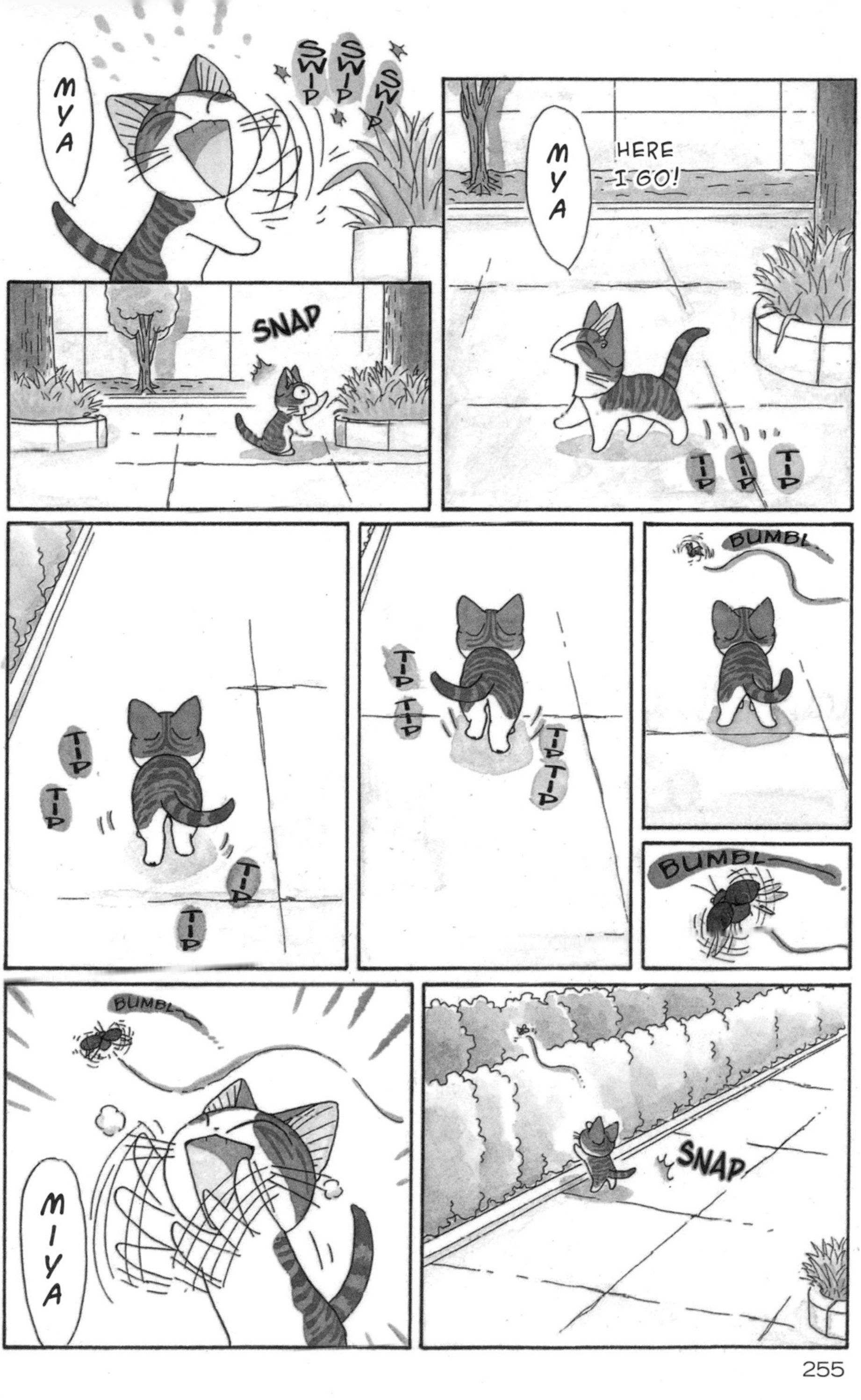

MYA
SWIP SWIP SWIP
SNAP
MYA
HERE I GO!
TIP TIP TIP
TIP TIP TIP TIP
TIP TIP TIP TIP
BUMBL
BUMBL—
BUMBL—
MIYA
SNAP

MYA
CHI IS OFF!
TIP TIP
FLUTTER
FLUT FLUT
FLUTTER
FLUTTER
FLUTTER
WHEE!
MIYA
MYA
WAIT UP!
POUNCE
SHOOM
OH!
MEOW
DASH—

YARGH!
SKRREECH
MYA?!
MEOW MEOW
NO!
MEOWR
DASH—
SKREEECH
WOAH!
THUD

CLOSE
NYA
THAT WAS CLOSE, HUH.
MIYA
OH!
MYA?!
NIYA
MAKE SURE TO ALWAYS LOOK BOTH WAYS.
NYA
SO WE MEET AGAIN.

MYA
WHATCHA UP TO?
NIYA
WHAT ARE YOU DOING ALONE?
MEOW
I'M GOING STRAIGHT AHEAD THAT WAY.
NYA
HURRY ALONG AND GO HOME NOW,
BEFORE YOU GET LOST AGAIN.
MYA
HRN?
AH, WHAT'LL WE DO WITH YOU?
NIYA
HERE GOES...
SHUMP
NYA
COME ALONG, NOW.
WHAT?

MYA?
WHERE ARE WE GOING?
NYA
I'M TAKING YOU HOME.
MYA
CHI CAN GO HOME ON HER OWN.
MYA HA HA HA
MEW
AND THIS ISN'T THE WAY ...
NIYA
YOUR MAMA MUST BE WORRIED.
LOST
MEE?
MA... MA?

the end

homemade 89: a cat visits

MA...
MA?
MA...MA
MAMA...
WHAT'S A "MAMA"?

MIYA
IS A "MAMA" SOMETHING FUN? IS IT A PWACE TO PWAY?
ENOUGH CHIT-CHAT, FOLLOW ME.
NYA
GWAR
EEP!
DASH—
LOST
WHY MUST CHI COME?
MYA
GRIPE
GRIPE
MYA
MYA
GRIPE
GRIPE
NYA
YOU LOOK SO MUCH LIKE YOUR MAMA, LITTLE ONE.

THIS "MAMA" LOOKS LIKE CHI?
MEOW?
NYA
YES
SHOOM SHOOM
POP
HEY HEY
MYA
DASH—
MIYA
IS IT BIG? IS IT SMAWL?
OF COURSE SHE'S BIG.
NIYA

BIG ...
SHOOM
SHOOM
HUFF
MEOW
BIG, HUH?
SKOOT——
NEOW
WHY OF COURSE SHE IS BIG.
BIG! BIG!
SHOOM
SHOOM
WOW...

NYA
WHAT A STRANGE ONE.
BE A GOOD CHILD AND MAMA GIVES YOU MILK.
NIYA
MIULK ?!
KITTEN MILK
OH!
DASH
MEOW
CHI WILL LOVE IT!

TRUE, ALL THE LITTLE ONES LOVE THEIR MAMA.
NIYA
MAMAS ARE SO BIG THEY CAN WRAP YOU UP WHOLE!
NYA
HM?
WRAP?
MYA
STUFFED.
ROLL ROLL
ROLL
WHAT?

HEY?
NYA
NYA
COME ALONG, QUICK.
SNAP
MYA
IS THAT TRUE?
SKAT
MEOW
CHI'S A LITTLE SCARED.
DASH——

NYA
NIYA
THIS IS AS FAR AS I'LL GO.
OH?
...
NIYA
BACK TO YOUR MAMA, NOW.

the end

homemade 90: a cat is reacquainted

THE "MAMA" ...
IS HERE?
IT GIVES MIULK.

SLURRRP SLURRRP
AHH!
BUT...
FWOP
MYA
KITTEN MILK
STUFFED.
NO ROLLY-SQUEEZIES, THANK YOU.
KLANG
KLANG
TIP TIP TIP TIP TIP
STILL...
THERE'S MIULK!
TIP TIP TIP TIP

BUT,
THE ROLLY-POLLIES!
TIP TIP TIP
WHAT TO DO?
BUT... MIULK!
TIP TIP TIP
PACE PACE
PACE PACE
!
I'LL DWINK THE MIULK.
SLURP SLURP SLURP SLURP
DASH—
AND THEN RUN!
GREAT IDEA!
HUP

MIULK PWEA...
MYA...
KREAK
STMP
STMP
STMP
!
STMP
EEK
DASH
SHOOM
FWOMP
STMP
OH NOS!

STMP
STMP
STMP
THE "MAMA" HAS LEGS!!
BETTER RUN!
FOOM
FOOM
HEY?!
SWIP SWIP SWIP
SWIP SWIP SWIP
SWIP SWIP SWIP SWIP
HUFF
HUFF

CHI GOT TWAPPED.
HELP ME!
HELP ME, DADDY!
HELP ME, MOMMY!
YOHEY!
...
ANYONE HEWLP!
SOMEONE ...
ANYONE PWEASE ...

LIFT
NYA
WHAT ARE YOU DOING HERE?
HUH?

NYA
THERE, NOW.
YO
NYAN
BLACKIE!

the end

homemade 91: a cat receives milk

CHI MISSED YOU!
MIYA
NYA
SO WHAT ARE YOU DOING HERE?
!
OH!
SHHH!

DASH——...
?
MYA
I'LL GIVE UP ON GETTING MIULK.
NYA?
MILK? FROM WHO?
SKOOT——
THE "MAMA"
MYA
SKOOT
MAMA?! YOU MEAN ...
NYU?
MYA
THE ONE THAT'S LIKE CHI.
SKOOT
PEEK
OH, THAT MAMA!
NYAN
DON'T YOU NEED TO SEE HER?
NYA?
HO
!
MIYA
MIYA
WHY SHOULD I?
"MAMA" IS HUGE AND WANTS TO CHASE AND WRAP CHI UP!
CHI
MYA
NO WAY.
...
HMM, SOME-THING'S WRONG.

BUT, MIULK...
MEE
MIULK
MEE
COME WITH ME.
NYA NYA
YOU MIGHT GET MILK.
MIULK!
MYA
DASH—
MIULK
MEOW
SKOOT

PLOP
SHFF
SHFF
HUFF
HUFF
HUFF
NYAN
I'M HOME.
NYAN
HOW 'BOUT SOME GRUB.
MEOW

MIYA
THANKS FOR THE MIULK.
LAP LAP
LAP LAP LAP
SMAK
LAP LAP LAP
LAP LAP
AH!
I'M SHTUFFED!
MIYA
FLOP
BONK

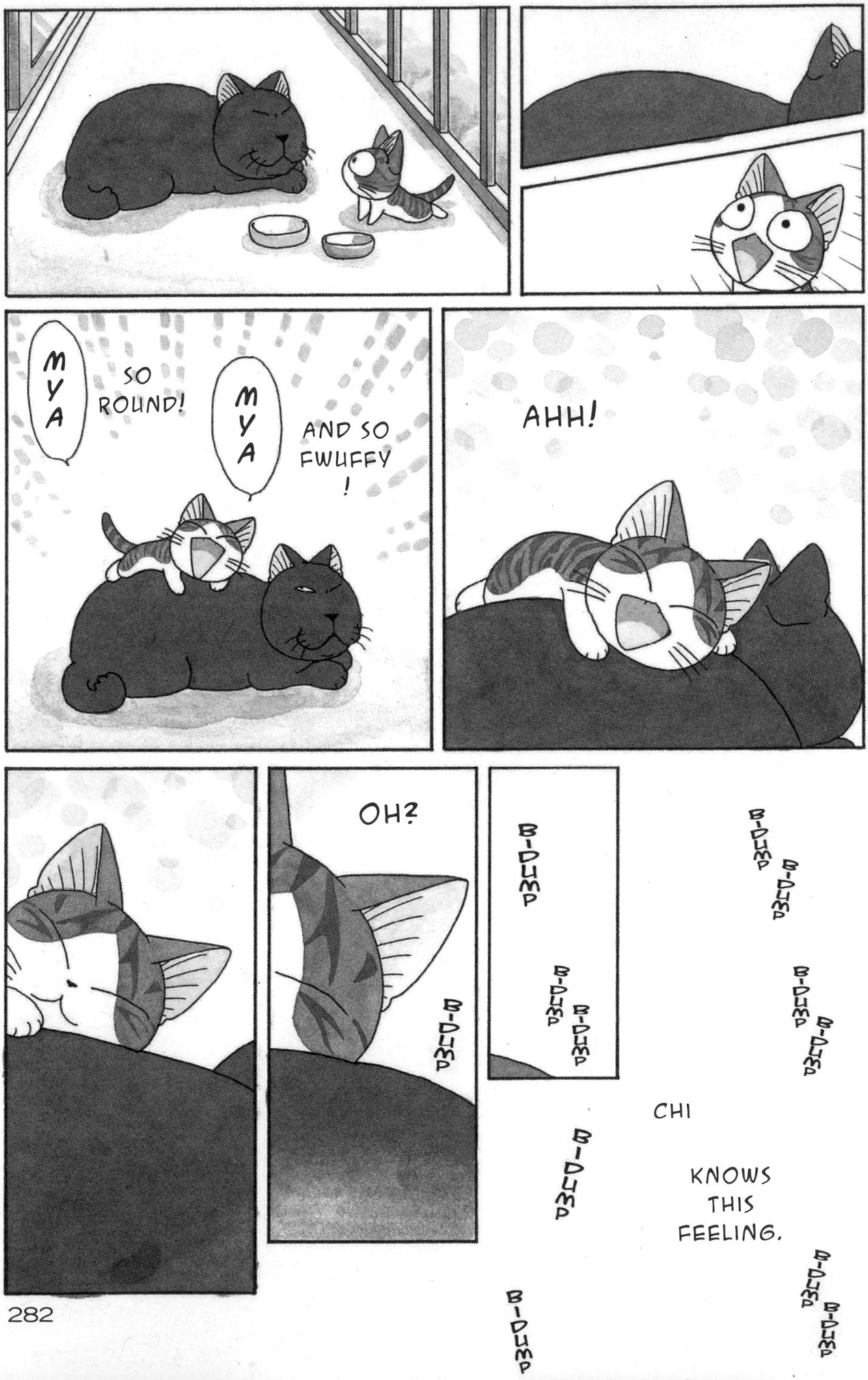

MYA
SO ROUND!
MYA
AND SO FWUFFY!
AHH!
OH?
BIDUMP
BIDUMP
BIDUMP BIDUMP
BIDUMP BIDUMP
BIDUMP BIDUMP
CHI KNOWS THIS FEELING.
BIDUMP
BIDUMP
BIDUMP BIDUMP

BIDUMP
BIDUMP
BIDUMP
THIS FEELING...
BIDUMP
BIDUMP
BIDUMP
BIDUMP
BIDUMP
WHAT WAS IT?
BIDUMP
BIDUMP
BIDUMP
WHAT WAS IT?
AHH
BIDUMP
DIDUMP
BIDUMP
CHI WAS DOING THIS...
BIDUMP
BIDUMP
BIDUMP
BIDUMP
BIDUMP

BIDUMP
FWUFFY, COMFY-WOMFY...
BIDUMP
BIDUMP
BIDUMP
WHAT WAS IT ?
RIGHT,
I GOT
MIULK, TOO.
NUZZL NUZZL
NUDGE

the end

homemade 92: a cat is directed home

NYA?
NEW HOME?
YUP!
MYA!
CHI WALKED A LOT TO GET HERE.
MIYA
HEH HEH
AH...
NYAN

WHICH WAY IS HOME?
NYA
WHICH?
NYU?
...
...
HAH...
I SAW AUNTIE CALICO...
MYA...
THERE WAS GWASS...
MEE...
AND BUGS...
MEE...
AND THEN,
MEE...
NYAN
WHAT WAS ALONG THE WAY?
NYA?
CALICO?

THIS WAY ?
MYA?
NYA
MAYBE
TIP TIP TIP TIP
NYA
THERE'S A WALL AUNTIE CALICO OFTEN SLEEPS ON.
GAZE GAZE
MYA
OH YEAH?
DASH—
BUMBL
DASH—
OH, WE'RE HERE!

YOU KNOW YOUR WAY FROM HERE?
NYA
MIYA
IS IT CLOSE?
UNYU
YEAH
MYA
IT'S STILL A LONG WALK.
HEH HEH HEH
NYU
FAR...
MYA
DOES BLACKIE WANNA COME ALONG?
... NYU
YUP.
MEOW
IT'S THIS WAY!
TIP TIP TIP
HALT
CHI FELL DOWN HERE.
MEOW
NYA
DID YOU NOW.
SMAK SMAK
NYU
LET'S GO.
IT'S THIS WAY.
MEOW
TIP TIP TIP

TAP
TAP
TAP
TIP
TIP
TIP
TIP
HALT
MIYA
THE SKWEE CAME HERE.
NYU
HN?
MYA
IT WENT SKWEE,
MYA
THEN WHAM!
UNYA?
AND WHAT ABOUT HOME?
MEOW
IT'S THIS WAY!
TAP
TAP
TAP
TIP
TIP
TIP
TIP
HALT
CHI FOUND A LEAF OVER HERE!
MYA
MYA
IT FLUT-FLUTTERED!
NYU?
SO...?
NYA?
HM?

NYU
THIS IS YOUR HOME?
HALT
OH?
MEOW
TAP TAP TAP
TIP TIP TIP TIP
MYA
THIS WAY!
TAP TAP TAP
TIP TIP TIP TIP TIP TIP
MYA
I SAW A BUG HERE!
NYU!
AND YOUR HOME ?!
MYA!
RIGHT!
HA LT
MEOW
IT'S THE GWASS!
...

SKOOT
MYA
YAY!
DOES SHE REALLY KNOW HER WAY BACK?
MYA MYA
HEY, OVER HERE.
MEOW
HERE! I'M GOING UP!
TAP TAP
NYU
WHAT NOW?
SHA
ZHA
VOOM VOOM

WOOSH
NYU
LATER, THEN.
MYA
I'M HOME!
CHI WALKED AROUND A WHOLE LOT!
MYA
TAP
TAP
TAP
TAP
TAP
TAP...
IT'S ACTUALLY PRETTY CLOSE IF YOU JUST GO STRAIGHT.
NYU

the end

homemade 93: a cat leaves her mark

HUH?
TIP TIP TIP
ARGH!

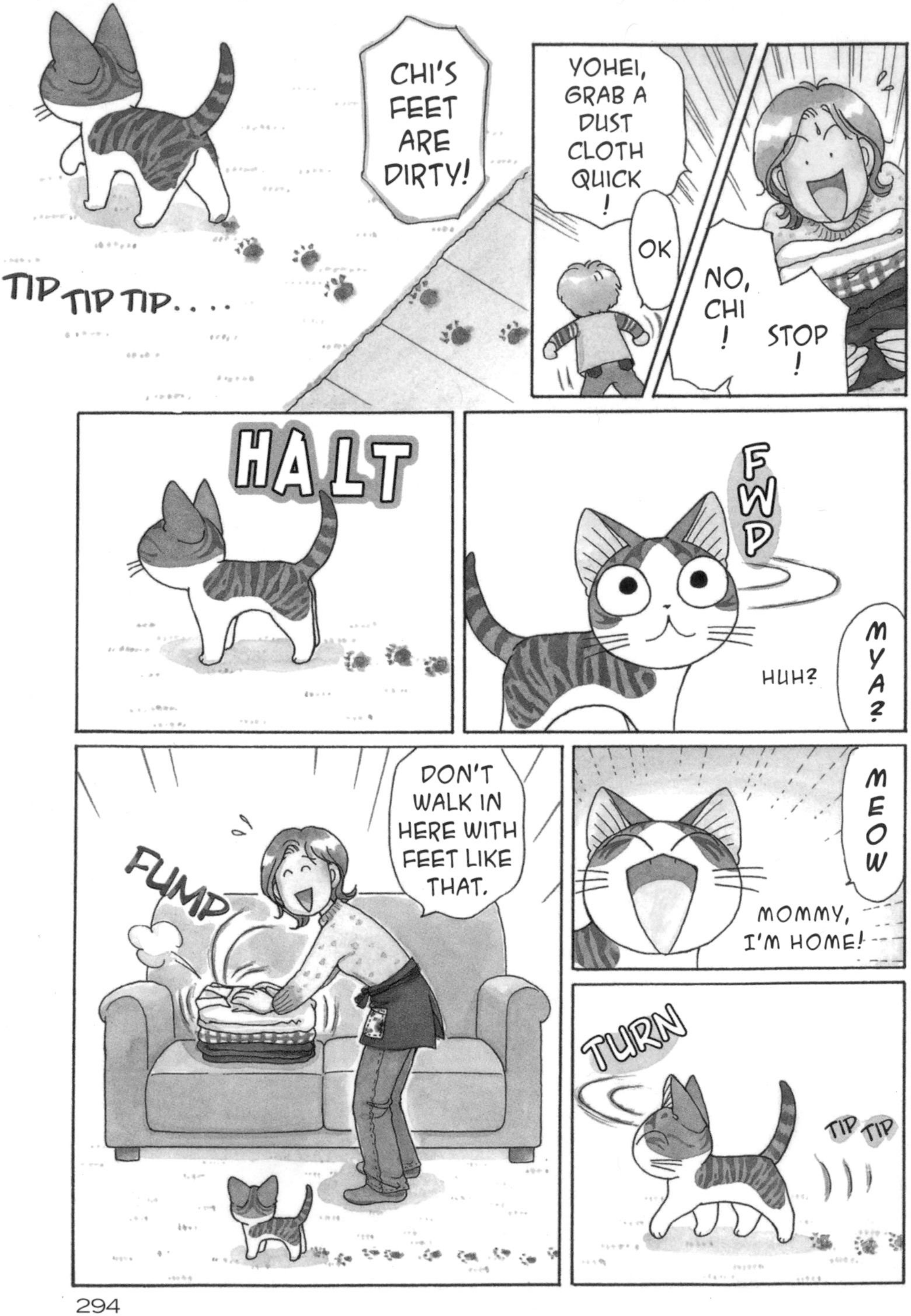

TIP TIP TIP....
CHI'S FEET ARE DIRTY!
YOHEI, GRAB A DUST CLOTH QUICK!
OK
NO, CHI!
STOP!
HALT
FWP
MYA?
HUH?
FUMP
DON'T WALK IN HERE WITH FEET LIKE THAT.
MEOW
MOMMY, I'M HOME!
TURN
TIP TIP

HEY, I SAID STOP!
UH
SKOOT
CHI, WAIT!
SHUMP
HOP
DASH
* SIGH *
TIP
TIP
TIP

I'VE GOT IT, MOM!
PLACE IT DOWN IN CHI'S PATH.
OK
TIP TIP TIP
TIP TIP TIP
WHAT'S THIS?
HEY?
MYA?
WALK ON THAT, CHI, YES?
RIGHT HERE, CHI.

THMP
TIP TIP TIP . . .
HEY !
CHI PASSED IT.
TIP TIP TIP . . .
TIP TIP TIP
OVER HERE !
TMP
TIP TIP TIP
HERE !
THMP
TIP TIP TIP TIP . . .

HALT
SHFF
SHFF
FWID
...
MYA?
WHAT'S THE MATTER?
WE'VE GOT NO CHOICE BUT TO CATCH HER.
ROLL
ROLL
GOT-CHA!
HUH?!
HUP

RUN AWAY!
MIYA
DASH—
FWAP FWAP
WHAT'S WRONG, MOMMY?!
MEOW?!
DASH—
SKFF
OH!
NO, NOT THERE!
SPROING
WHMF
I'M HOME!

AN ESCAPE ROUTE!
HA HA HA...
HEY
THIS STUFF CAN BE CUTE EVERY SO OFTEN.
GOES THIS WAY...
AND THIS WAY...
THEN
SHE ENDED UP HERE?
YUP.
ON YOUR SHIRT.
HEH
the end

homemade 94: a cat is stopped

MYA?
WHAT'S THIS?
REACH

YARGH!
ZING
MYA?
NOT THAT!
THIS IS REALLY HOT STUFF!
YANK
TUNK
PHEW
THAT WAS CLOSE!
FWEE
FWEE
REACH
FWEE
WOAH

STOP THAT!
NO!
THE IRON IS
BAD!
MOMMY'S A HOGGER.
FLOP
THUNK
WHAT'S THIS?
NICE
I WANTED TO PUT THIS SPACE TO USE.
HONEY
TMP TMP

GWAR
HI-YAA
MEOWR
SMAK SMAK
SMAK SMAK
MEOW
HAH!
PO-THOS?
YEAH.

THEY'RE EASY TO CUL-TURE.
OUR HOME COULD LOOK PRETTY GREEN.
SOUNDS LIKE FUN!
CHOMP
CHOMP
CHOMP
CHOMP
CHOMPCHOMP
CHOMP
THE PO-THOS !!
ARGH!
HN?
IT'LL GO EXTINCT BEFORE IT EVEN HAS A CHANCE!
AND CHI'S CHEWING IT. IS IT EVEN EDIBLE?

LET'S SEE, FLORA CATS SHOULD AVOID ARE
AMA-RYLLIS, ALOE ...
MIYA
MIYA
MAR-GUERITE, PRIMULA, JASMINE,
POTHOS AND OTHERS ...
CAT
PO-THOS?
MEOW MEOW
NO! NO!
BAD!
PO-THOS BAD!
DADDY'S HOARDING THAT.
I DIDN'T REALIZE BUT
THERE ARE MANY DANGERS FOR CHI AROUND.
GNAW
GNAW GNAW
BAD!

PLASTIC TABS
DETER-GENT
TIDIER
TIDIER
THREAD
AND SMALL POINTY ITEMS.
SHE KNOCKS VASES DOWN
AND CHEWS AND PLAYS
WITH ALL SORTS OF STUFF.
TIP TIP TIP....
IT'S LIKE WHEN YOHEI WAS A BABY.
YEAH
LET'S PLACE DANGER-OUS ITEMS
OUT OF REACH.
WOAH

MOM
CHI'S IN TROUBLE!
WHAT?!
THERE WAS ANOTHER DANGEROUS ITEM?
THIS IS CHI'S!
KLUTCH
AT LEAST IT'S NOT DANGEROUS, SO WE BEST LET IT GO.
YUP
JUST A NUISANCE...
YAY! CHI CAN HOG THIS!
MEOW

the end

homemade 95: a cat battles
TIP
TIP
TIP
TIP
ARK
WHAT'S THAT?

STARE
PREY?
KLUK
P-R-E-Y!
KLUK
KLUK
GRIN
SLINK SLINK
TUT
HUH
TUT

TIP TIP TIP
TUT TUT TUT
TIP TIP TIP TIP
TUT TUT TUT TUT
SKAT——..
SKOOT——..
PANT
PANT
PANT
PANT
CAN'T CATCH IT.
GLANCE
HALT
HERE'S MY CHANCE!

TWINGE
TWINGE
KLUK
SHOOM
HOP
KLUCH
HEY!
!
TUT
POWNCE
HOP
KLUCH
TUT

HOP
POUNCE
HOP
POUNCE
HOP
POUNCE
TURN
HOW CAN IT TELL I'M BACK HERE?
!
HOO
HOO
HOOOOO
?
HMM?

HOO
HOO
TUT
TUT
TUT
TUT
HOOO
OH, I'M GONNA GET YA!
SMIRK
CHI'S GONNA JUMP YA FROM THE SHADOWS!
TWINGE
TWINGE
SPROING

MEOWR
THIS TIME
CHI'S GONNA
WIN!
FLAP
FWAP
MYA?!

FW
AP
MEOWꝹ!
PANT
PANT
...
CHI LOST.

the end

homemade 96: a cat appears

HOO
HOO
PREY!
UP HIGH ...
A WHOLE BUNCH.

STMP STMP STMP
STMP
MEOWR
EEP!
STMP STMP STMP STMP
HOW ABOUT HERE?
YEAH!
MYA
I SEE!

MIYA
CHI'S GONNA FIND A NICE SPOT TOO.
WHERE WOULD BE GOOD?
TAP TAP TAP
SHOOM
KREAK
SHOOM
KREAK KREAK
WHMP
MYA
THIS AWEA IS NO GOOD.
SKOOT
TAP TAP TAP
WHERE'S A GOOD PWACE?
MYA
MEOW
OH, I'VE FOUND ONE!

TTTKU
TTTKU
TTTKU
MIYA
THIS IS CHI'S PWACE!
HUH?
I'M IN THE SHADE.
TAP TAP TAP
OH!
THAT LOOKS WARM!
HM?

MEOW
I CAN'T CWIMB IT.
FWAP
FWAP
FWAP
AH!
MEOW
NOW ISN'T THIS NICE!
MYAR
ZHAK
ZHAK
ZHAK
ZHAK
THERE MUST BE A GOOD SPOT.
TIP
TIP
TIP
PING
HUFF
HUFF
HUFF
HUFF
MEOW!
WOAH!

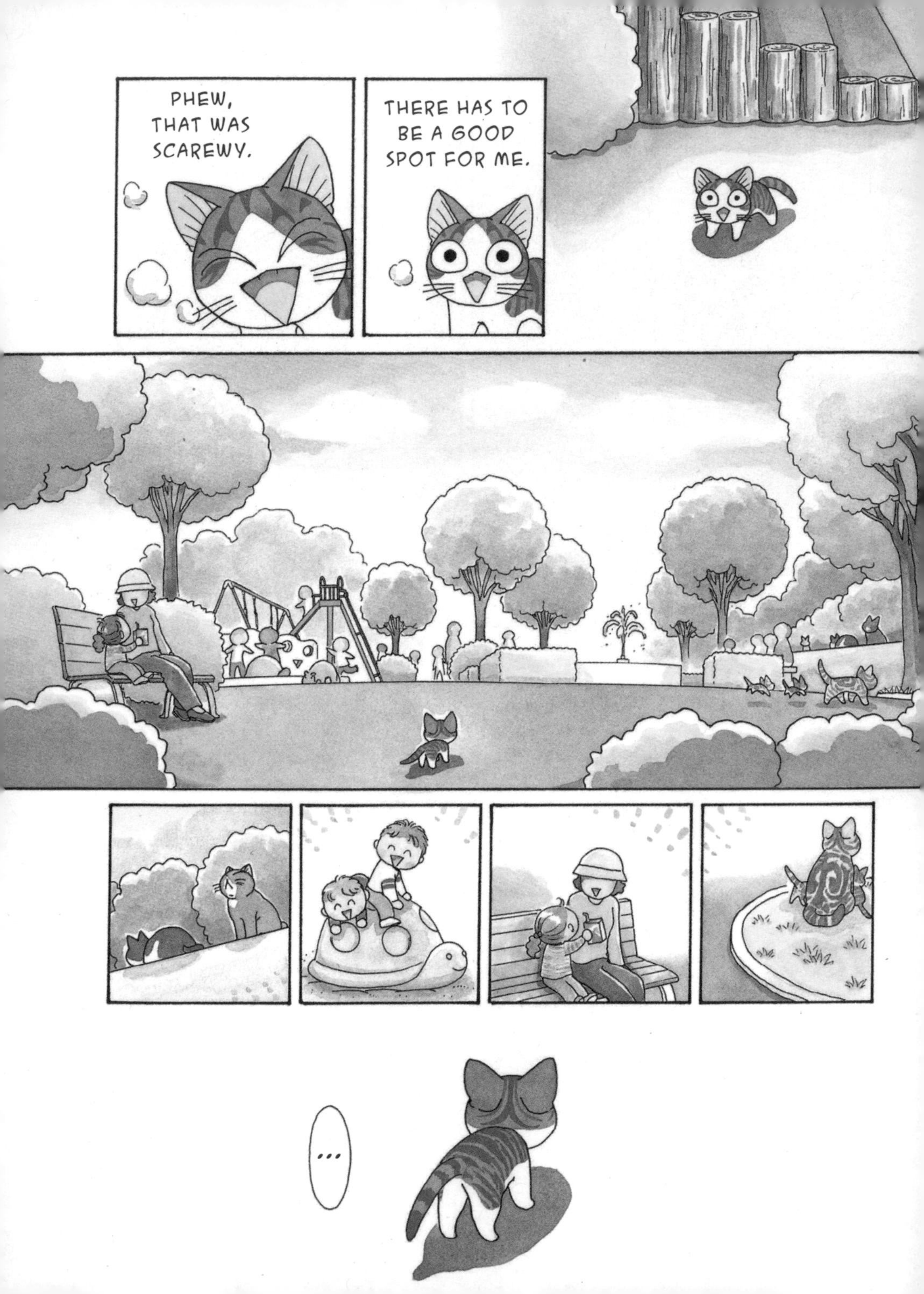
PHEW, THAT WAS SCAREWY.
THERE HAS TO BE A GOOD SPOT FOR ME.
...

SPLOOSH
SPLOOSH
PLIP
PLIP
PLIP
HEY?

MYA?!
HUH?!
MRR
TSK
SPLOOSH

the end

homemade 97: a cat beckons

STARE
SNFF SNFF SNFF
I'LL CHECK THIS ONE OUT FIRST...

SMIRK
GRIN
MEOW?
DIDJA COME HERE ON YOUR OWN?
CHI'S LOOKING FOR A NICE SPOT.
MIYA
AND THIS MIGHT DO...
MYA
MRR
HAH, IT WON'T.

MEOR
THIS BE MY TURF, SO GET OUT!
WHY'S THAT?
MYA
THIS PUNK'S A RUNT,
LOOKS WEAK
AND HAS A STUPID FACE.
MEOW
LET'S PLAY TOGETHER!
MYA
COME ON...
SKREE SKREE SKREE
GOTS NO JUMPING SKILLS EITHER.
GLID GLID
SNORT
BAH, GAME OVER!
HMPH
MIYA
YAY, I CWIMBED IT!
MYA
HEY

MEOW
YOU'RE PWETTY SMALL!
MIYA
WHAT SHOULD WE PLAY?
PLAY WITH THIS ONE?
MEORG
GAPE
DON'T MESS WITH ME!
MREOG
GAPE
THERE! HAD ENOUGH YET?
EEP!
MYA
MYAMYA
RUN AWAY!
DASH—
HOP

HEH, THAT WAS A SNAP!
HUFF
PANT
HUFF
HUFF
HUFF
SO MUCH FUN !!
HUFF
PEEK
FWIP
SNEAK
MEOW
I'M OVER HERE!
WOOSH
POP
WOOSH
WHA?!

POKE
WOOSH
TAP TAP TAP---
MRR
WHAT NOW?
CREEP
THRILL
GLOMP
MYA!
MRR
MRG
DASH

HA!
WAIT UP!
MIYA
SKOOT—
SKAT—
SKOOT~
SKKF....
TURN
HALT
MYA
RUN!
MIYA
HOLD UP!
MRR
MIYA
MIYA
SKOOT—
SKAT—

MRR
MIYA
MIYA
MRR
HUFF
HUFF
PANT
HUFF PANT
HUFF
HUFF
PANT
PANT
MEOW
WHAT A BWAST!
MIYA
PLAYING TOGETHER IS SO MUCH FUN, HUH?
PLAYING... TOGETHER?
HUFF
HUFF
ME?
I PLAYED... TOGETH-ER?
SPLOOSH

the end

homemade 98: a cat is satisfied

HOW COULD I?!
NOT WITH THIS ONE!
MEOW
WHAT YA WANNA PLAY NOW?
MIYA
HEY, COME ON
TSK

SORRY TO SAY,
MERR
MEORG!
BUT THIS HERE BE MY TURF.
LEAN
MRR
SO GET OUT!
TMP
WHAT KINDA GAME IS THIS?
MYA
MRR
THIS AIN'T NO GAME!
GAPE
AND I'M A BUSY GUY.
MRR
HRMPH
OKAY THEN,
MEOW
MEOW
CHI'S GOING HOME!
IT WAS FUN!
MIYA
MIYA
LET'S PLAY AGAIN, 'KAY?
SPRING
MYA
BYE-BYES!

HALT
TURN
SPLOOSH
THAT SURE WAS FUN!
AND HOME IS THAT WAY.

MYA
GOING HOME!
SPRO-ING
MYA
HOME!
MYA
GOING
MYAH
HOME!
BOING
BOING
BOING
AH!
MYA
MYAH
YAY!
BOING
MIYA
AHEAD
MIYA
AHEAD
MIYA
RUN!
SKID
SKID
SKID
RUN!
MEOW
SPLISH
DASH—

SKOOT— SKAT——
PLAYING TAG WAS SUCH A HOOT!
MYA WHAT
MEOW A
MIYA BWAST!
HOP HOP HOP
BARK BARK
HM?
RUFF RUFF
HEY?
OH!
MYA!
MIYA IT'S BARKS FROM NEXT DOOR!
YOU'RE CHI FROM NEXT DOOR.
RUFF WOOF

HEY BARKS, CHI—
MIYA
RUFF
SKOOT—
MIYA
WENT TO THE PARK!
PANT
RUFF
WOOF
MYA
CHI PLAYED.
SKOOT—
I GOT TO PLAY TAG!
MIYA
HUFF
YOU SURE MEOW A LOT...
WE PLAYED TOGETHER.
MEOW
HUFF
HUFF
HA
HA
SKOOT—
TOGETH-ER...
MYA
HEY?
MYA
I NEVER ASKED HIS NAME.
MEOW
HUFF
HUFF

PANT
HUFF
IT WAS FUN, THOUGH!
MEOW
HUFF
RUFF RUFF
PANT
PANT
PANT
PANT
MYA
PANT
OH, RIGHT!
PANT
I BETTER TELL YOHEY ABOUT THIS!
PANT
PANT
PANT
MEOW
I'M HOME!
PANT
PANT
PANT
PANT
PANT
YOHEY, YOHEY
MYA
MYA
PANT
PANT
PANT
PANT
PANT
PANT
AH, CHI.
LAP LAP LAP LAP LAP
AHH!

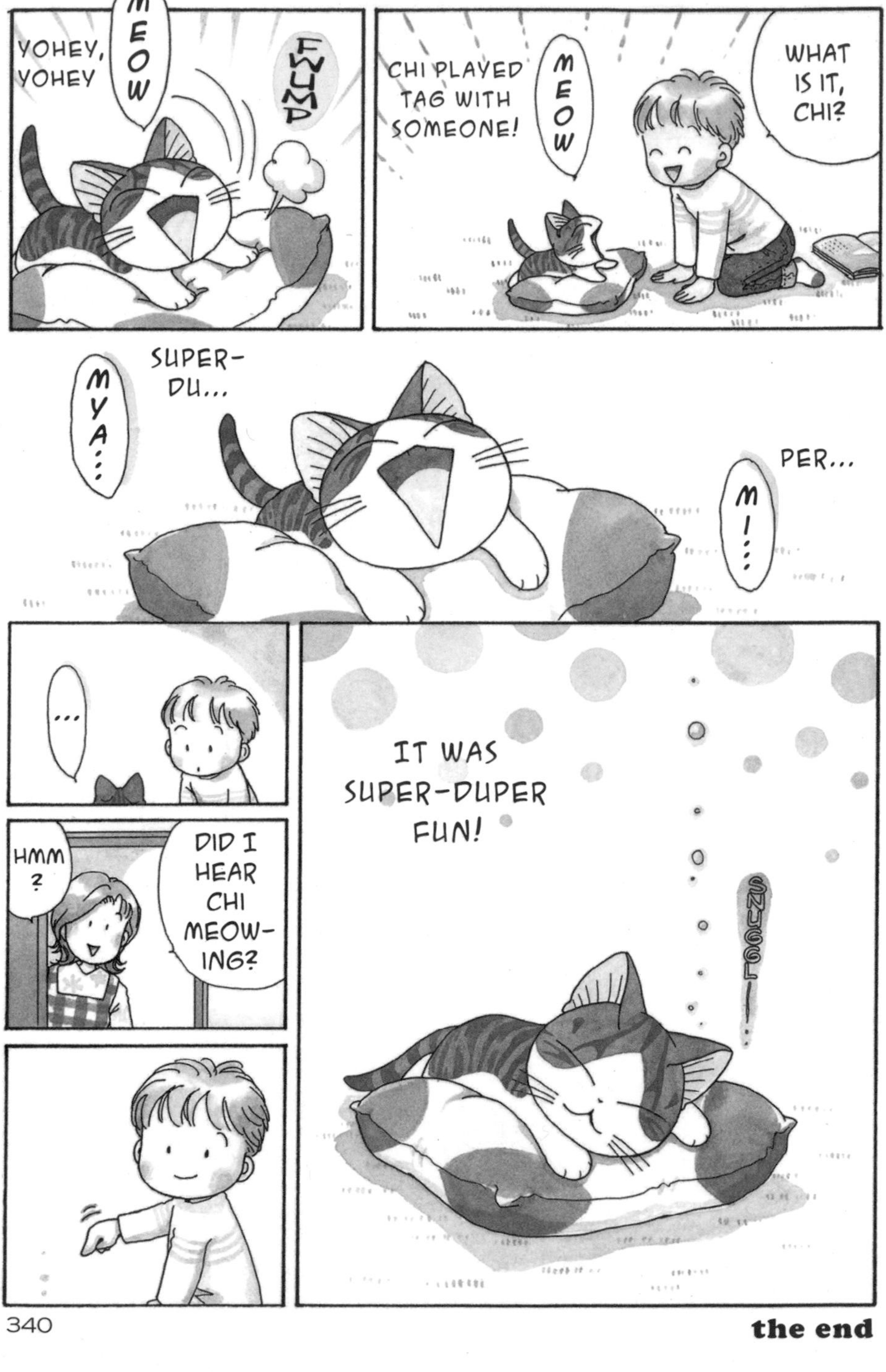
WHAT IS IT, CHI?
CHI PLAYED TAG WITH SOMEONE!
MEOW
YOHEY, YOHEY
MEOW
FWUMP
MYA...
SUPER-DU...
PER...
MI...
...
HMM?
DID I HEAR CHI MEOWING?
IT WAS SUPER-DUPER FUN!
SNUGGL-

the end

homemade 99: a cat is pleased

RSTL
RSTL
WHAT
IS IT ?!
OH, IT'S SOME-THING GOOD!
RSTL
WHAT'S GOING ON?
CHECK IT! A VIDEO CAMERA!

BOUGHT ANOTHER GADGET I SEE.
HEY, CHI!
A VIDEO CAMERA!
SEE, CHI'S GLAD, TOO.
NICE!
MEOW
I'VE ALWAYS WANTED ONE OF THESE.
REACH
ZWASH
MIYA
IT'S CHI'S NOW!

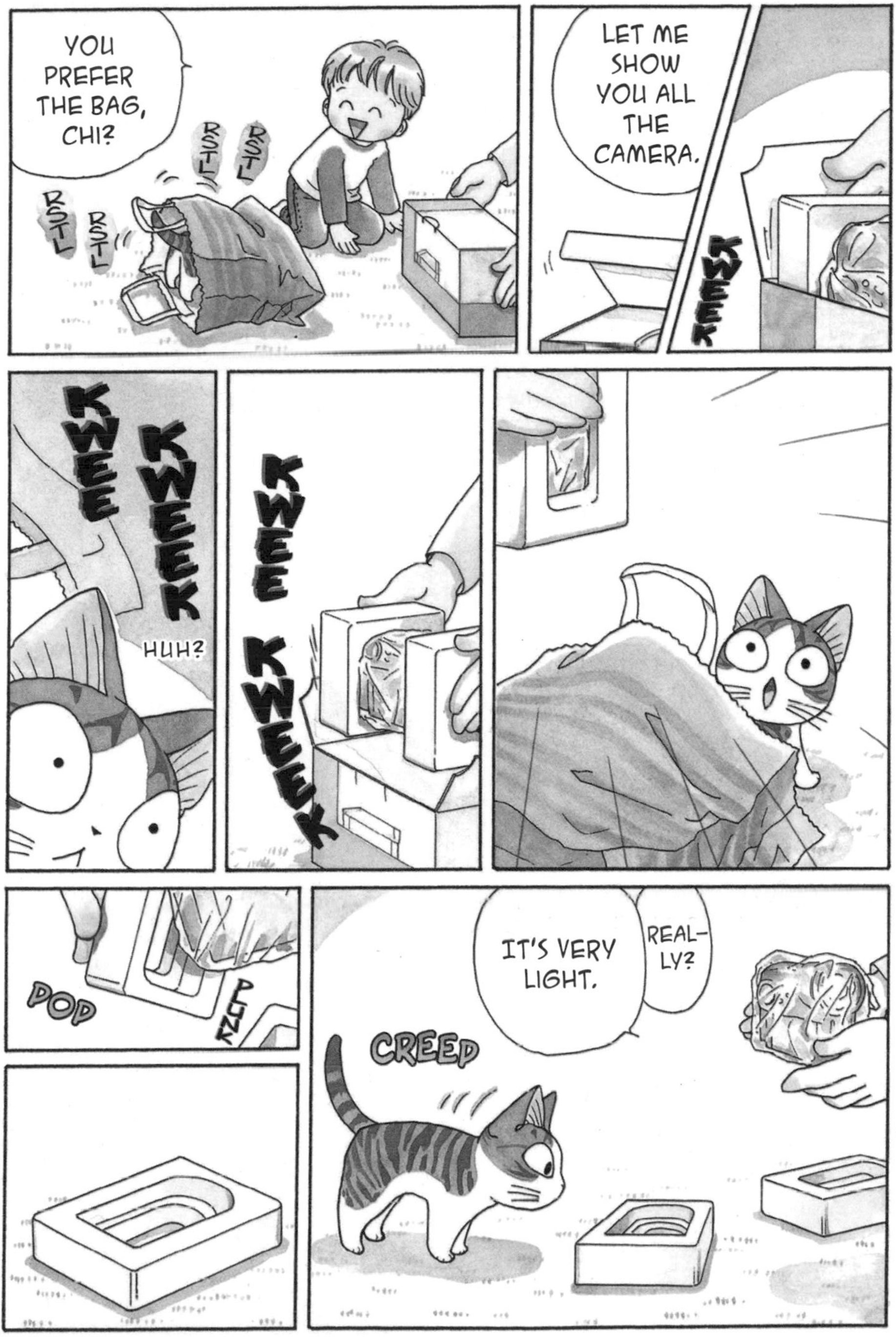

YOU PREFER THE BAG, CHI?
RSTL
RSTL
RSTL
RSTL
LET ME SHOW YOU ALL THE CAMERA.
KWEEK
KWEE
KWEEK
HUH?
KWEE
KWEEK
POP
PLUNK
IT'S VERY LIGHT.
REAL-LY?
CREEP

TAP
SMAR
SMAR
SMAR
GRIP
KLUNK
KLUNK
WOAH!
HUP, HUP.
HERE!
SEE?

SKSH
AND IT'S JUST AMAZING!
SKSK SKSK
SKSH SKSH
SKSH SKSH SKSH
THE IMAGE QUALITY IS GREAT, AND IT HAS HANDHELD IMAGE CORRECTION, TOO.
SKSK SKSK
SHMP
MEOW
PREY!
DASH—

VIDEOS WILL COME OUT GREAT ON THIS.
RIGHT, CHI?
I'VE CAUGHT THE PREY!
MEOW
HUH?
SO MUCH PACKAGING.
THIS TOO.
UHH, FORGET THE GARBAGE, CHI.
YO-INK
HEY?
MYA

PLOP
LOOK AT THIS!
WHAT'S THIS?
IT'S A VIDEO CAMERA.
COOL, HUH?
FLIT FLIT
FLIT FLIT
HALT

TIP TIP TIP TIP
SHOOP
SHOOM
SHOOM
SKSH
SKSH
SKSH
DADDY, DADDY—
MIYA
THIS IS GREAT!
MIYA
LOOKS LIKE CHI VALUES THESE MORE.

the end

homemade 100: a cat celebrates

HEY?
THE CAKE AND PRESENTS ARE READY.
I'M ALMOST DONE, TOO.
YOHEI'S GONNA BE SURPRISED!
THIS SHOULD BE FUN!
BETTER GET THE CAMERA READY.
TMP TMP TMP TMP

GRIP
SHFF
SHFF
WHAT'S THIS?
SLINK
SLINK
SLINK
SNFF
SNFF
SNFF
WHAT A NICE SMELL!

SHOOP
MUSH
LAP LAP
SO TASTY!
LAP LAP
LAP
LICK LICK
LICK
SMACK

MIYA
CHI'S MAKING THIS MINE!
PLAP
PLAP PLAP
PLAP PLAP PLAP
HN...
AHHH!
HUFF
CHI CAN'T EAT IT ALL!
OH?

WHAT'S THAT ON TOP?
NUDGE
MYA
OH, IT MOVES!
PUSH—...
SMUSH
MIYA
CHI MOVED IT!
AH!
WHAT ABOUT THAT ONE?
MEOW
SMOOSH
HRN?

MYA
OH, THIS ONE'S WOBBLY!
YANK
ROLL ROLL
TUNK
MEOW
I DID IT! IT FELL!
HUH?

MEOW
REALLY?
SOMETHING FUN?
WHAT IS IT?
HA HA HA!
IT'S A FUN CELEBRATION!
AND I THINK IT MIGHT BE TIME TO START.
SNAP
CAMERA BATTERIES SET!
HMM, NO IDEA...
I CAN'T WAIT.
MYA
MYA
MYA
MYA
OH!

MEOW
WHAT A BWAST!
WHAT'S GOING ON?
WAAAAA !!
HAPPY BIRTHDAY YOHEI
YO ... YO-HEI
HAPPY BIRTHDAY!
KLIK
...
HAPPY BIRTHDAY YOHEI

the end

homemade 101: a cat shares

DREAM RAIL
E ARE AWAY
NOT ANSWER
E BELL.
S ARE IN THE FRIDGE
REAM, TOO!
WHAT'S THAT, YOHEY?
MIYA

OH!
MIYA
I AND 2...
KLAK
KLAK
KLIK
CHI TOO!
MEOW
MYA
GO, GO!
MYA
SKRT
SKRT
SKRT
MEOW
I DID IT!
KLAK
KLAK
AH!
STOP THAT, CHI!
SHUV
DON'T BREAK IT, OKAY?
MEOW
CHI WILL PLAY TOO!
DRAT
OH?!

MIYA
SO MANY IN HERE.
KLIK
KLIK
RTTL RTTL RTTL
RATTLE
RATTLE
GRID
CHI!
MEOW!
MIYA
THIS IS CHI'S SPOT!
PUSH PUSH
SHUV
GET OUT OF MY WAY!
WHATCHA DOING!
MEOW
MOVE IT, CHI!
MEOW
MEOW
PUSH PUSH
PUSH
SHUV

SHFF...
SHFF...
I'LL DO THIS AWAY FROM CHI.
MIYA
DON'T YA GET INTO CHI'S SPACE!
KLIK
KLIK
KLIK
KLIK
SHFT
KLAR
SHFT
KLAK
YAY!
I DID IT!
UH...
SFHT
KLAR
KLAR
DE-PART
KLAK

SHFT
KLAK KLAK
SHFT
KLAK
CHI GOT ACROSS!
MYA
MIYA
MANY TIMES!
KLAK KLAK
SHFT
KA-TUNK KA-TUNK
KA-TUNK
KA-TUNK KA-TUNK
KA-TUNK ...

SIGH
...
!
CHI ... CHI ?!
CHI ?!
MEOW

OVER HERE!
MYA
CHI'S OVER HERE!
MIYA
KA-TUNK KA-TUNK
MEOW MEOW

TWEET
HEY, A SPARROW!
PREY!
MIYA
NUZZLE NUZZLE NUZZLE
WHAZZAT?
RUSTLE RUSTLE
MYA
SNACKS!
MYA?
ICE CREAM
SHUK
PLOP
WE'RE HOME!
TASTY, HUH.
MIYA
TASTEY, HUH.

the end

homemade 102: a cat is sucked

FOOM!...
FOOM
FOOM
SKOOT OVER, CHI.
FOO
MYA?
I'M VACUUMING, SO MOVE OVER?
FOOM!...
FOOM
FOOM

FOOM!
FOOM!
IT'S GOING "FOOM"!
MIYA
YOU'RE IN MY WAY.
FOOM!
FOOM!
YOINK
THMP
HEY, CHI WAS PLAYING THERE!
MIYA
HATING VACUUM CLEANERS.
SO MUCH FOR CATS
FOOM

WHAT CAN YOU DO?
MYA
SLUMP
FOOM
FOOM...
FOOOF...
MOVE, CHI!
FOOM...
FOOOM...
MEOW
CHI'S SHLEEPING HERE!
FOOOM
YOINK
FOOM...

THIS IS TAKING SO MUCH TIME.
THERE'S SO MUCH FUR TO CLEAN UP.
FOOM
FOOM!
HRN
GRIP
CHI ISN'T MOVING ANYMORE.
HRMPH
SHOOM...
CHI... MOVE.
SOOM...
I'VE GOT TO VACUUM THERE, TOO.
SOOM!

MYA
CHI'S NOT MOVING.
USE OF FORCE?
GRIP
PHEW
SHOOM
SHOOM!!
CHI, IF YOU DON'T MOVE, I'M GONNA SUCK YOU UP.
POKE POKE
SHOOOM
SHOOOM!!
!

MEOWR
WHATCHA DOING, MOMMY!
SHOOM!
MOVE
SEE, SEE?
HEY...?
SHOOM...
AH?!
SHOOM!
HUH?
SHOOM
SHOOM!...
WHAT?
MIYA!
SHOOM...
OH!

A VACUUM BRUSH!
WOW
SHOOM
LOOKS LIKE SHE'S TAKEN TO THE BRUSH NOZZLE.
SHOOM
WHA?
CHI LIKES TO BE SUCKED BY THE VACUUM?!
THE WOO-WOO BWUSH FEELS SO GOOD.
MEOW
SHOOM
SHOOO...
AH!
AS YOU BRUSH,
YOU CAN ALSO CLEAN UP THE CAT HAIR!
SHOOM
AWE-SOME!
WON-DERFUL!
PRRR.
PRRR
PRRR

FOOM!!...
SISH
FOOM!!...
GLAD YOU LIKE IT...
FOOM!!...
MIYA
MIYA
MIYA
BUT THIS ...
FOOM!!...
THRILL
SKAMPER
FLOP
FOOM!!...
THIS ISN'T ANY EASIER.
MEOW
DO IT, DO IT, MOMMY!
FOOM!!...
SKAMPER
FOOM!!...
PLOP

the end

homemade 103: a cat tosses

KA-CHUNK
BOY, IS MY CRAFTMANSHIP GOOD!
HA HA HA
MEOW
WHAT YOU GOT THERE, DADDY?
BOD

HUH?
MYA?
TUNK
TUNK
TUNK
TUNK
TUNK
TUNK
TUNK
TUNK
TUNK
TUNK
TUNK
TUNK
WOW

WHAT ABOUT THIS ONE?
MYA?
KLAK KLAK
SHOOM
BONK
BONK
BONK
BONK
BONK
KLUNK
BONK BONK
BONK

WOAH! AMAZING!
BAMF
KLUNK
KLUNK
KLUNK
FALL! FALL!
MEOW
03
WHUMP
WHUMP
WHUMP

ROLL ROLL
WOOHOO! COOL!
THIS ONE'S GOTTA FALL, TOO!
MEOW
MIYA
FALL, FALL—
MYA
FALL, FALL—
IT DOESN'T WANNA MOVE.

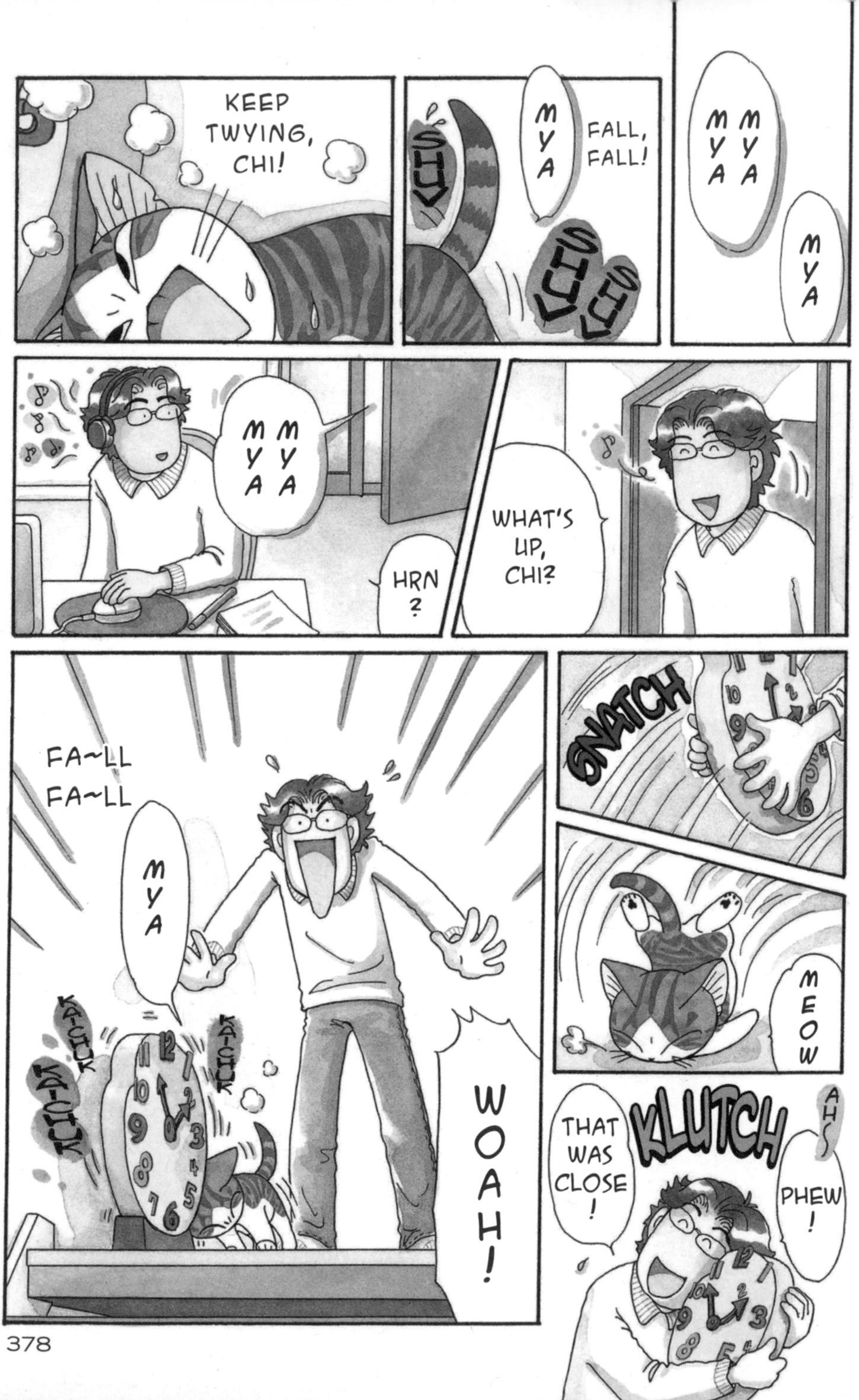
KEEP TWYING, CHI!
SHU
MYA
FALL, FALL!
SHU
SHU
MYA MYA
MYA
MYA MYA
HRN?
WHAT'S UP, CHI?
FA~LL FA~LL
MYA
KA-CHUK
KA-CHUK
KA-CHUK
WOAH!
SNATCH
MEOW
KLUTCH
THAT WAS CLOSE!
AH~
PHEW!

HM?
TUMBL TUMBL
HUH?
MIYA
MYA
ROLL
OH
CHI, WATCH OUT!
GRIP

ARGH !!
WHONK
WHONK
WHAM
BLAM
THUD
THE HEAVY THING FELL!
MEOW
YOU'RE SO STRONG!
MIYA
UGH
YOU'RE AMAZING, DADDY!
MIYA

the end

homemade 104: a cat peeks

RUFF RUFF
WHAT'S BARKS FROM NEXT DOOR DOING?
MYA?
SHAK
LET'S SEE.
MYA
SHAK
ZHAK

DASH
MYA
WHATCHA DOING?
RUFF
SPIN
MYA
MIYA
I CAN'T SEE.
DASH

WHAZZAT?
MYA
WOOF
WHAT IS IT?
MIYA
TURN
HEY
MYA
SKRUF SKRUF SKRUF
SKOOT—
SHOW ME!
MEOW
!
STIFF
KLUCH

MIYA MIYA
WHAT IS IT?
WOOF WOOF
MIYA MIYA
WHAT IS IT? WHAT?
RUFF RUFF
MEOW MEOW
RUFF RUFF
CHI TOO, CHI TOO!
GRIP
WHY NOT?
!
RIGHT!
TIP TIP TIP
SHAR
SHAR
SHAR

SKUF
SKF
SKF
SKFF
GRIN
HE'LL DROP HIS GUARD, AND I'LL GET IT!
TWITCH
TWITCH
STRETCH
HEY?
HUFF
HUFF
PANT
SKFT
SKFT
SKFSKFT

HUFF
SKFF
HUFF
SKFF
HA
SKFF
RUFF
HA
HA
HUFF
SHAK
...

WAS THAT SOMETHING SPECIAL?
OH...
WAS THAT SOMETHING SPECIAL FOR BARKS?
MYA?

...
NOD
SHF
SHF
SHF
...
TIP TIP TIP TIP

the end

homemade 105: a cat opens her heart

IT'S TUFFY-FWUFFY SIS.
WHAT'S SHE UP TO?

STARE
?
MYA
WHAZZAT?
MIU
WATER
MYA
WATER?
SHOOM
MYA
WAIT, YOU'LL GET WET!

DON'T INTERRUPT ME.
MIUUU
GLARE
GOT-CHA
MYA
FWIP FWIP FWIP
PLIP
SPLAT
SWIP SWIP SWIP SWIP
MYA
CHI'S ALL WET NOW!
MEUWN
MYA?
HUH?
HM?

MEOW?
IS THERE SOMETHING GOOD IN THERE?
SPRING
NOTHING.
MEUWN
WOW
HM?
WAS THERE SOMETHING?
PLIP
SWIP
SWIP
SWIP
?
?

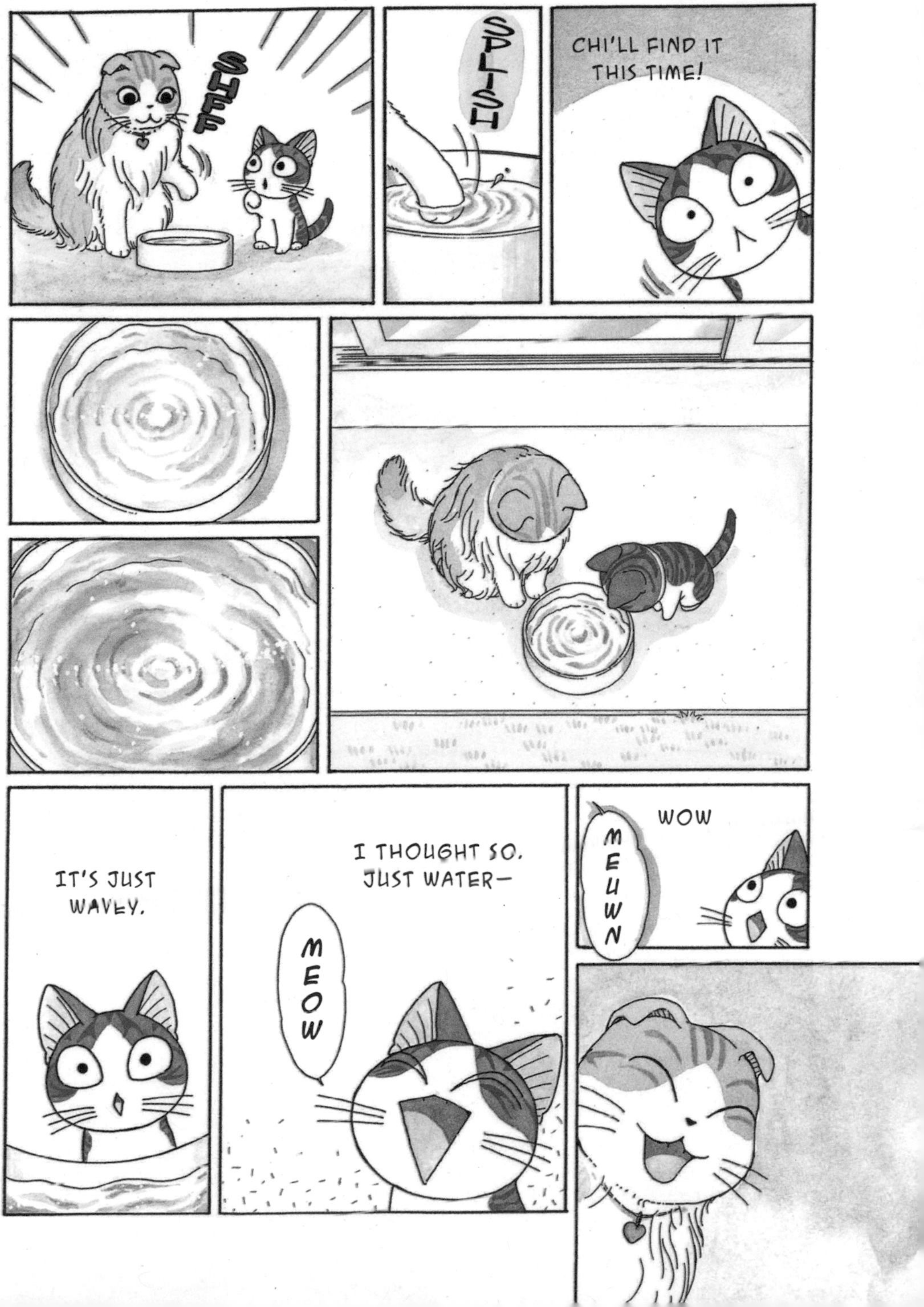
SHFF
SPLISH
CHI'LL FIND IT THIS TIME!
IT'S JUST WAVEY.
I THOUGHT SO. JUST WATER—
MEOW
WOW
MEUWN

SHE'S SMILING.
SMILING?
GRIP
HE WAS SMILING, TOO.
HE HAD—
HAD...
SPLISH
SOMETHING SPECIAL.

NOT JUST WATER.
SPECIAL.
IT'S ALL WAVEY, HUH?
MYA
YEAH, I LOVE THIS.
MIUN
SPECIAL, WAVEY WATER.

MIUN
WANT TO DRINK WITH ME?
HUH?
MYA?!
FWIP FWIP
CHI CAN HAVE SOME, TOO?
TUFFY-FWUFFY'S SPECIAL WATER?
MIYA
MIU?!
HUH?
MIYAN
IT'S JUST WATER.
...
MIU
AND IT'S ALICE, BY THE WAY.
NYA
NYA
NYA
NYA
LAP LAP LAP LAP LAP
TASTEY WATER!

the end

homemade 106: a cat is copied

TWEET
TWEET
TWEET TWEET
PREY!
THERE'S PREY!
MIU
MIYA
HMM, I WONDER.
MEOW
CHI'S SURE OF IT! PREY!

SHAK
SHAK
SHAK
ZHAK
TWEET
TWEET
TWEET
TWEET
TWIRTLE
TWEET
TWEET
I'VE COME TO HUNT.
I KNEW THERE'D BE PREY.
IT'S GOING "TWIRTLE."

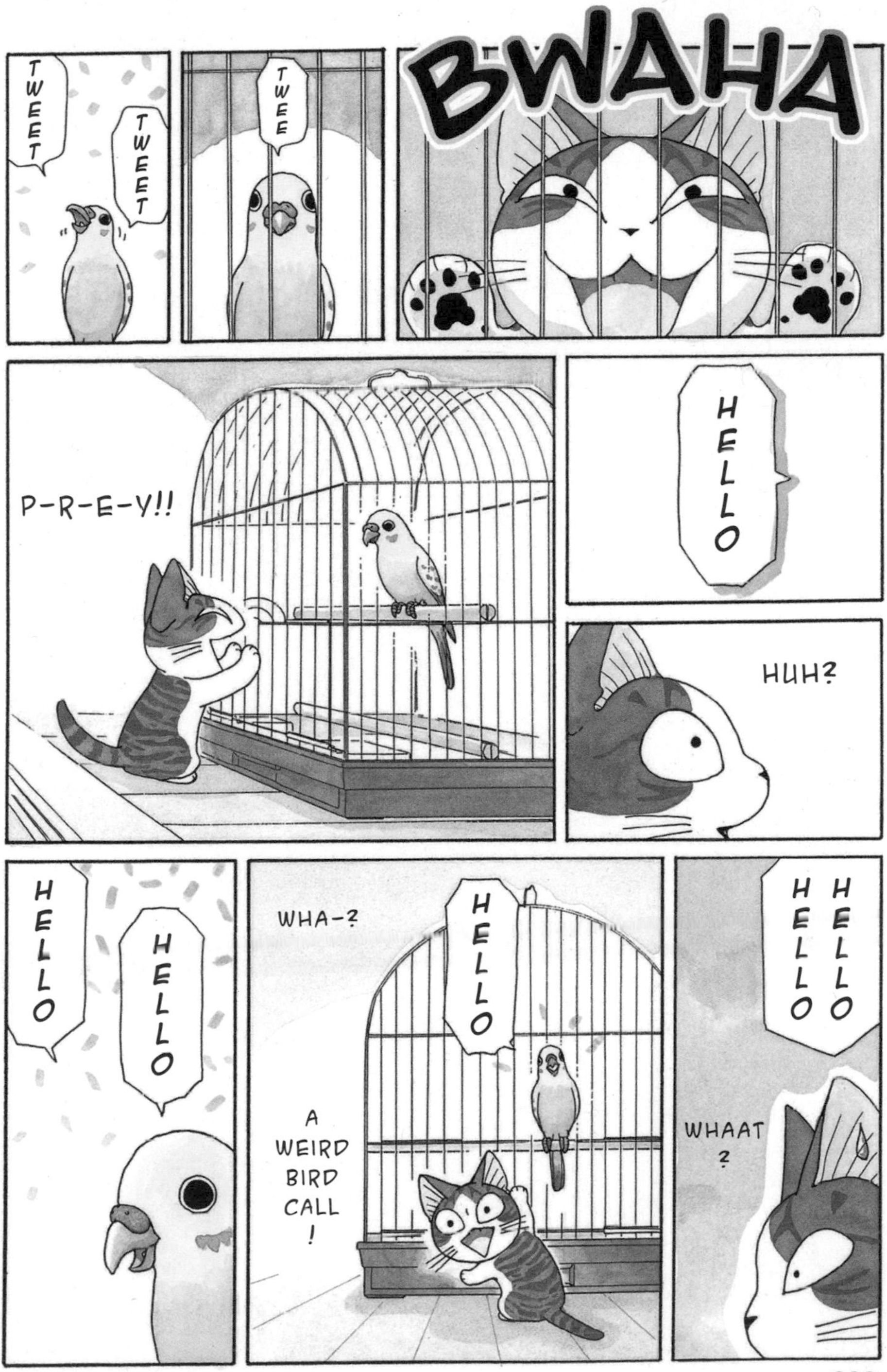
TWEET
TWEET
TWEE
BWAHA
P-R-E-Y!!
HELLO
HUH?
HELLO
HELLO
WHA-?
HELLO
A WEIRD BIRD CALL!
HELLO HELLO
WHAAT?

MEOW
WHAT?
HELLO
MEOW
WHAT?
HELLO
MEOW
WHAT?
MEOW
WHAT?
MEOW
WHAT?
TWITCH
TWITCH
TWITCH
TWITCH
MEOW
WHAT?

MEOW
WHAT
MEOW
WHAT
HUH?!
?!
WHAT
MEOW
WHAT
MEOW
HUHHH?
IT'S SAYING "WHAT" TO CHI?
BUT WHY?
CALM DOWN
GET A GRIP, CHI.
WHAT
MEOW
FWIP

MIYA
WHAT'S GOING ON?
MIYA
WHAT'S GOING ON?!
TWITCH
TWITCH
TWITCH
TWITCH
TWITCH
HRN?
MIYA
WHAT'S GOING ON

CHIRP
CHIRP
CHIRP
CHIRP
MIYA
MIYA
WHAT'S GOING ON
WHAT'S GOING ON
MIYA
WHAT'S GOING ON
...?
CHI
WHERE ARE YOU?
CHI
DASH—

WHAT
MYA
DASH—
WAS
MYA
DASH—
THAT?!
MYA
DASH—
PANT
PANT
PANT
PANT
PANT
HEY,
IT'S CHI!
MYA
I'M—
I'M HOME!
MYAR
WOULD YOU LIKE A SNACK, CHI?
IT'S MILK.
MMYA MMYA
I THINK I'LL PACK IT UP FOR TODAY.
LAP
LAP
LAP
LAP

the end

homemade 107: a cat accepts

TIP TIP TIP TIP TIP TIP TIP
TINK
IT'S A COLLAR FOR CHI.
IT'S GOT A BELL.
AND A NAME TAG, TOO.
CHI
IT TOOK ME FOREVER TO PICK THIS.
HA HA HA
IT'S SO CUTE.
MYA
WHAT'S THAT?

YO, CHI.
THIS IS YOURS.
I'M SURE IT'LL SUIT HER.
I CAN'T WAIT!
MEOW
WHAT, WHAT?
CHI
WRAP
HUH?
THRILLED
SNAP
HUH?
MYA
HUH?
SO CUTE!
...
?
TINK

SWIP SWIP SWIP
SWIP
SWIP
TINK TINK TINK TINK TINK TINK
PLINK
TINKLE
CHI
MIYA
I TOOK IT OFF!
THE COLLAR'S TOO BIG.
I FORGOT TO ADJUST TO HER SIZE.
HOW ABOUT THIS?
WRAP
HUH?
CHI
MEOW
WHAT'S GOING ON, DADDY?
SNAP
TINKLE
CHI

IT'S SO CUTE, CHI!
KLAP KLAP
...
CHI
SWIP
TINK
SWIP SWIP SWIP
TINK TINK TINK TINK
SWIP SWIP SWIP SWIP SWIP
TINK TINK TZ--- TZ---
IT WON'T COME OFF.
MYA
COME OFF!
SWIP SWIP SWIP SWIP
TINK TINK TINK TINK
ALMOST THERE.
SWIP SWIP TINK TINK
TINK TZ---
KDG
UH?!

WHAT'S THE MATTER, CHI?
MEGWAR
TINKLE
CHI
OH NO, SHE'S SNAG-GED UP.
MGAW
TINKLE
TINKLE
MGAW
MGAW
TINKLE
TINKLE
MGAW
ARGH
WE'VE GOT TO TAKE IT OFF.
DASH—
MGAW
WAIT, CHI!
DASH-

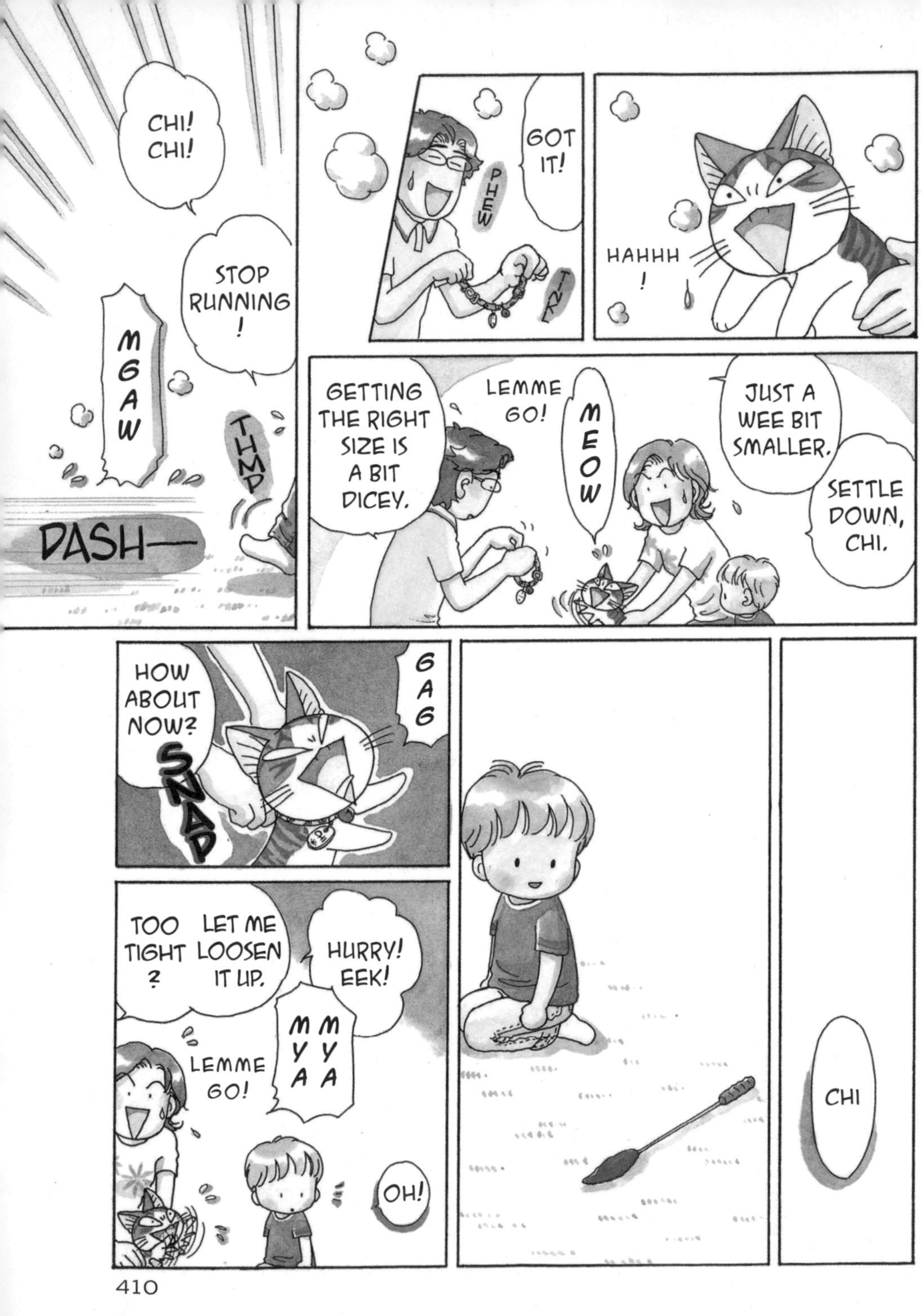
CHI! CHI!
STOP RUNNING!
MGAW
THMP
DASH—
PHEW
GOT IT!
TINK
HAHHH!
GETTING THE RIGHT SIZE IS A BIT DICEY.
LEMME GO!
MEOW
JUST A WEE BIT SMALLER.
SETTLE DOWN, CHI.
HOW ABOUT NOW?
GAG
SNAP
TOO TIGHT?
LET ME LOOSEN IT UP.
HURRY! EEK!
MYA MYA
LEMME GO!
OH!
CHI

FWIP
FWIP
FWIP
WOAH
MEOW
LET'S PLAY!
OK, HERE GOES!
SNAP
HUH?
HM?
STARE
H-HOW ABOUT NOW?
CHI

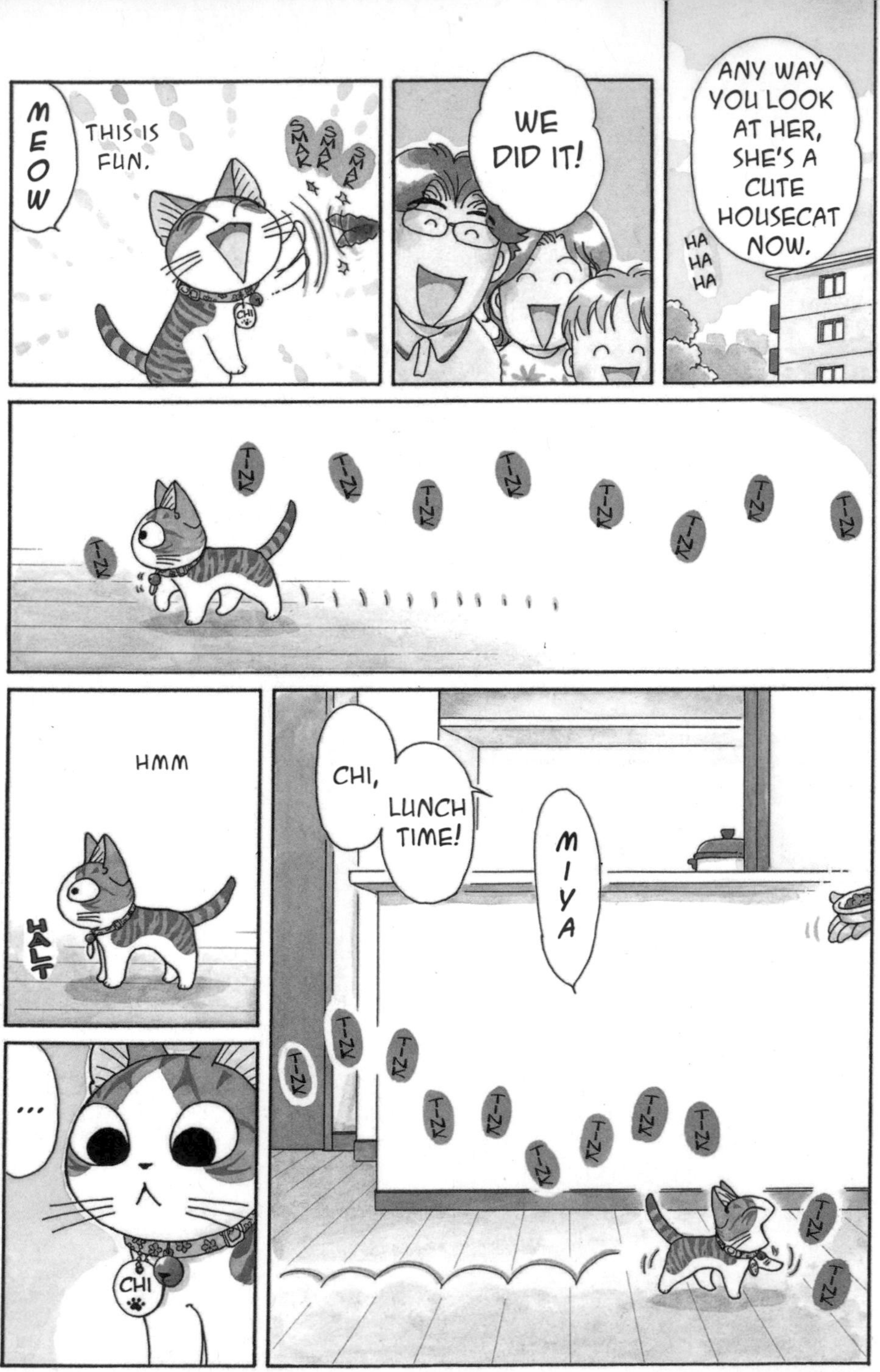
MEOW
THIS IS FUN.
SMAK SMAK SMAK
WE DID IT!
ANY WAY YOU LOOK AT HER, SHE'S A CUTE HOUSECAT NOW.
HA HA HA
TINK TINK TINK TINK TINK TINK TINK TINK TINK
HMM
HALT
CHI, LUNCH TIME!
MIYA
...
CHI
TINK TINK TINK TINK TINK TINK TINK TINK TINK TINK TINK
CHI

the end

homemade 108: a cat saunters

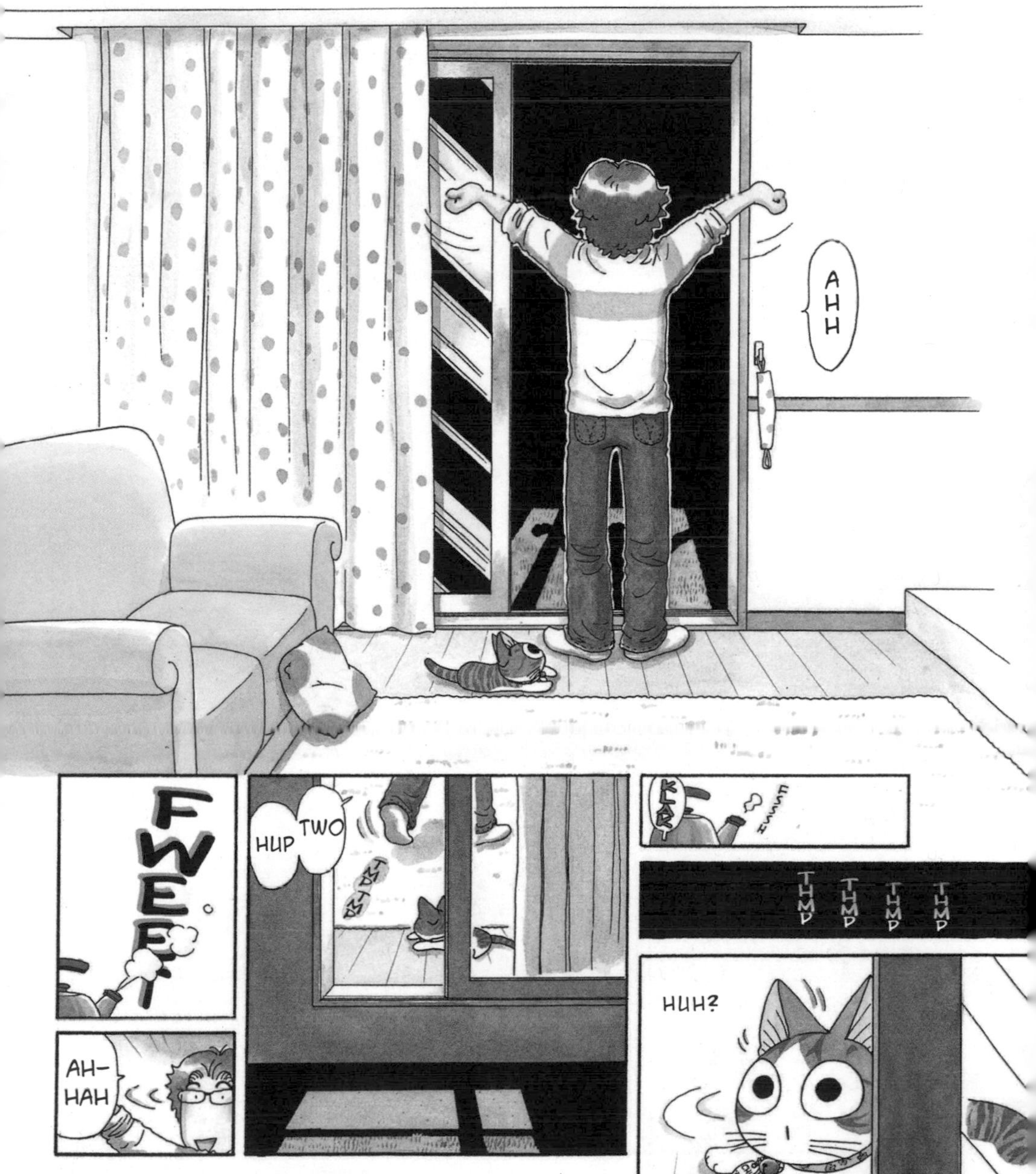
AHH
FWEET
HUP
TWO
AH-HAH
THMP THMP THMP THMP
HUH?

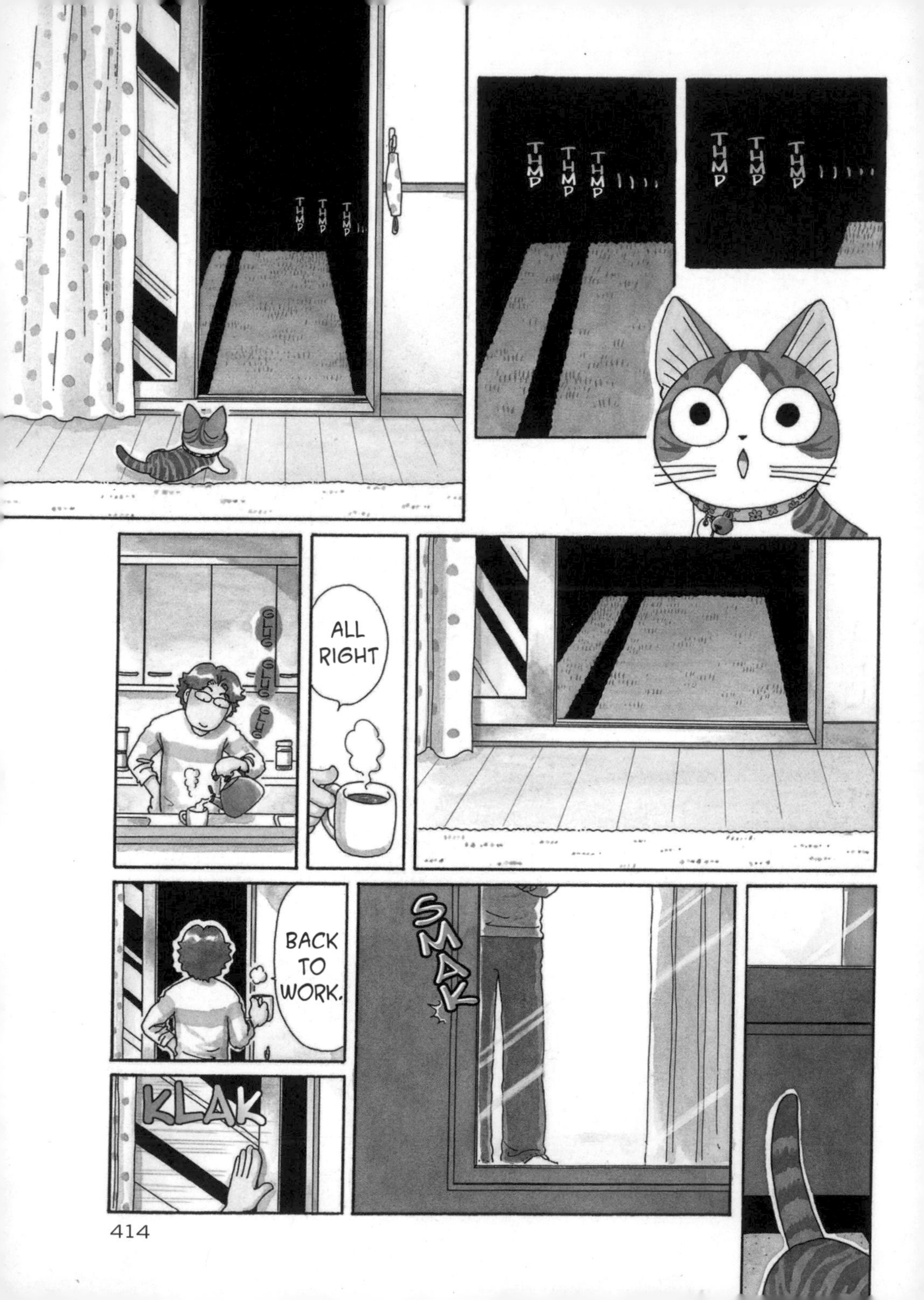
THMP THMP THMP
THMP THMP THMP
THMP THMP THMP
GLUG GLUG GLUG
ALL RIGHT
BACK TO WORK.
KLAK
SMAK

THMP THMP THMP
WHAT'S GOING ON?
THMP THMP
GRIN
TINK
TINK
THMP THMP THMP
TINK TINK TINK
TIP TIP TIP
THMP THMP THMP
TINK TINK TINK
TIP TIP TIP
TINK TINK TINK
TIP TIP TIP TIP
TUMP
HALT
?!
TURN

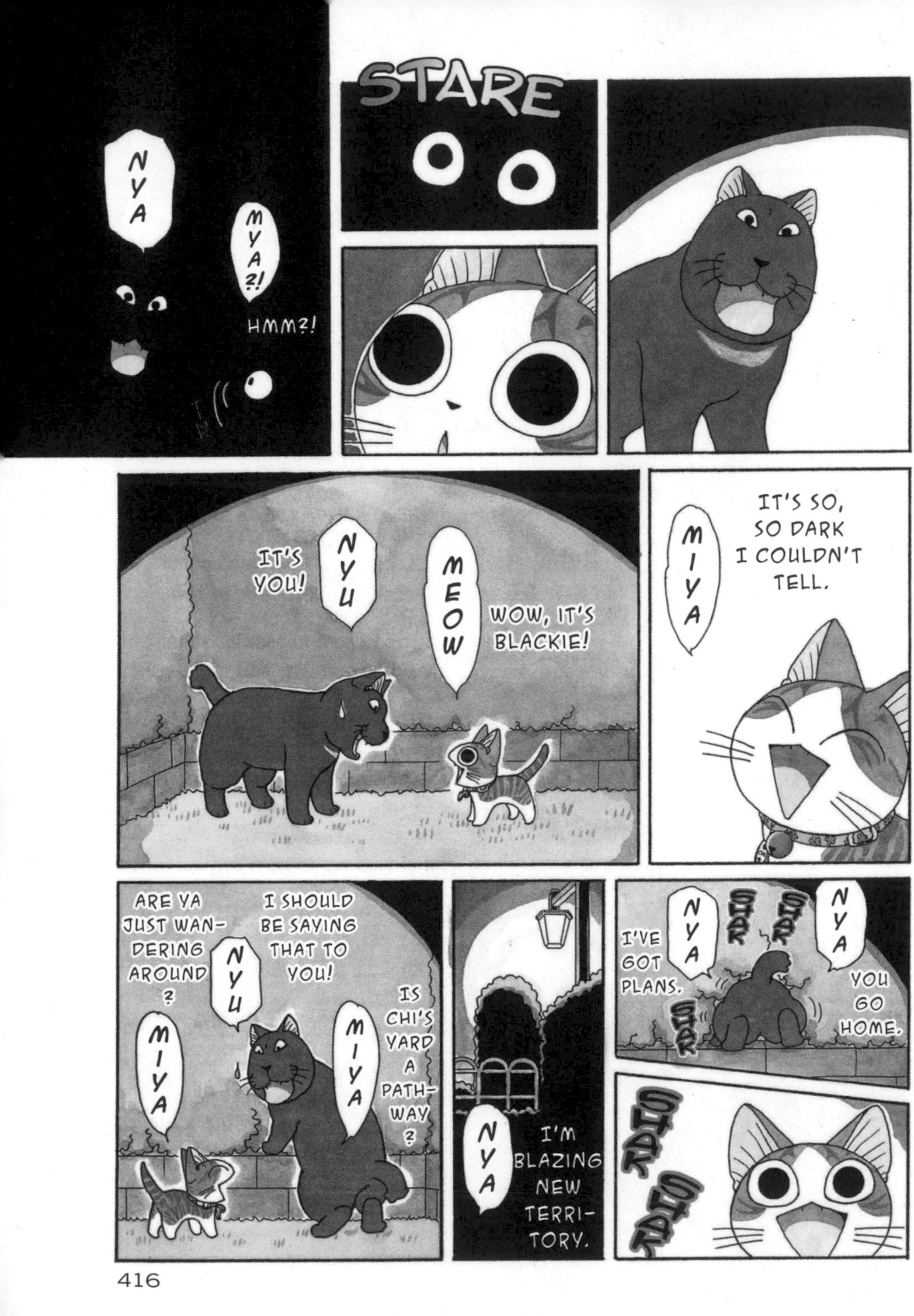
NYA
MYA?!
HMM?!
STARE
NYU
IT'S YOU!
MEOW
WOW, IT'S BLACKIE!
MIYA
IT'S SO, SO DARK I COULDN'T TELL.
NYU
ARE YA JUST WAN-DERING AROUND?
MIYA
I SHOULD BE SAYING THAT TO YOU!
MIYA
IS CHI'S YARD A PATH-WAY?
NYA
I'M BLAZING NEW TERRI-TORY.
NYA
I'VE GOT PLANS.
SHAR
SHAR
SHAR
NYA
YOU GO HOME.
SHAR
SHAR

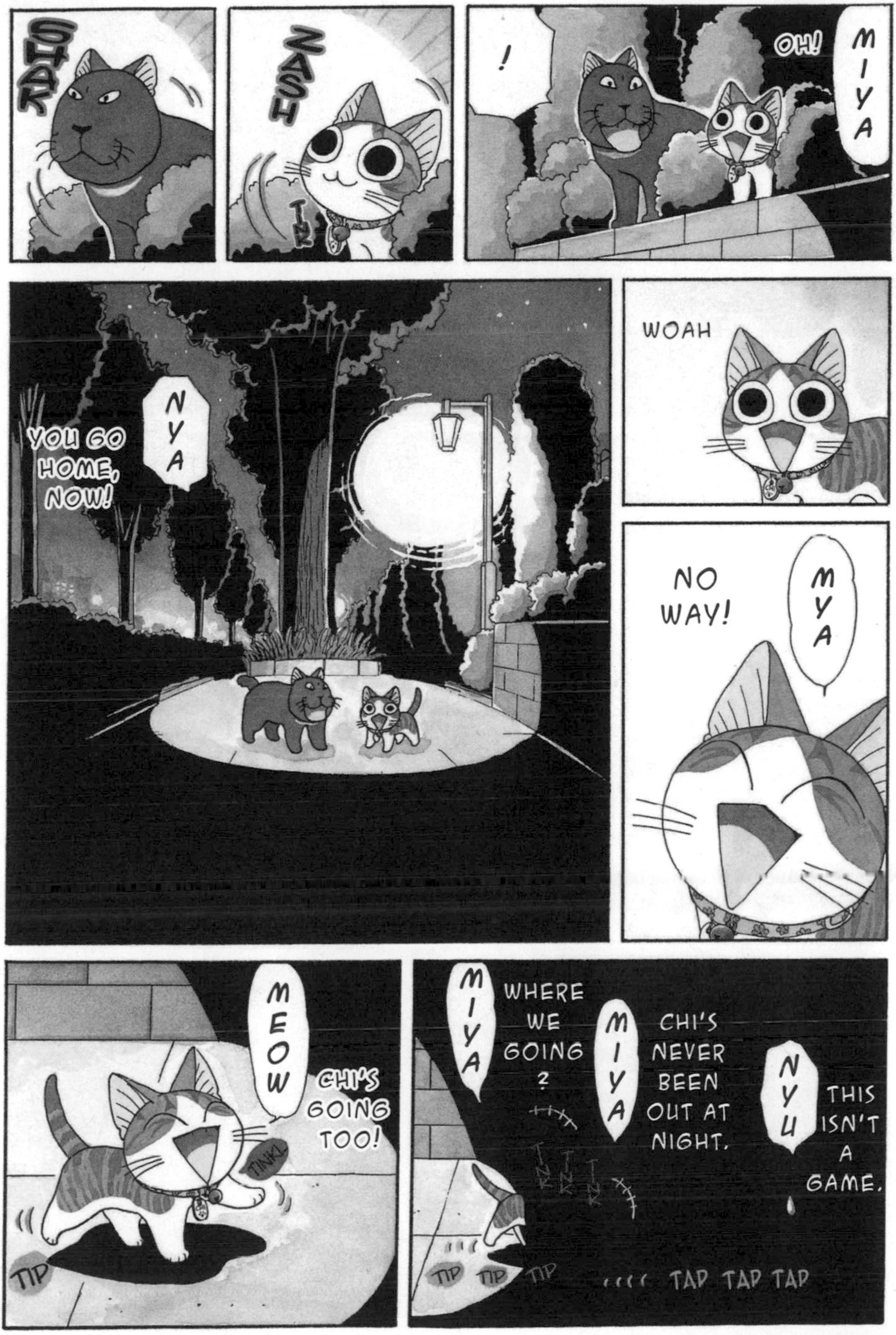

SHAR
ZASH
TINK
!
OH!
MIYA
WOAH
NYA
YOU GO HOME, NOW!
NO WAY!
MYA
MEOW
CHI'S GOING TOO!
TINKL
TIP
MIYA
WHERE WE GOING?
MIYA
CHI'S NEVER BEEN OUT AT NIGHT.
NYU
THIS ISN'T A GAME.
TINK TINK TINK
TIP TIP TIP
TAP TAP TAP

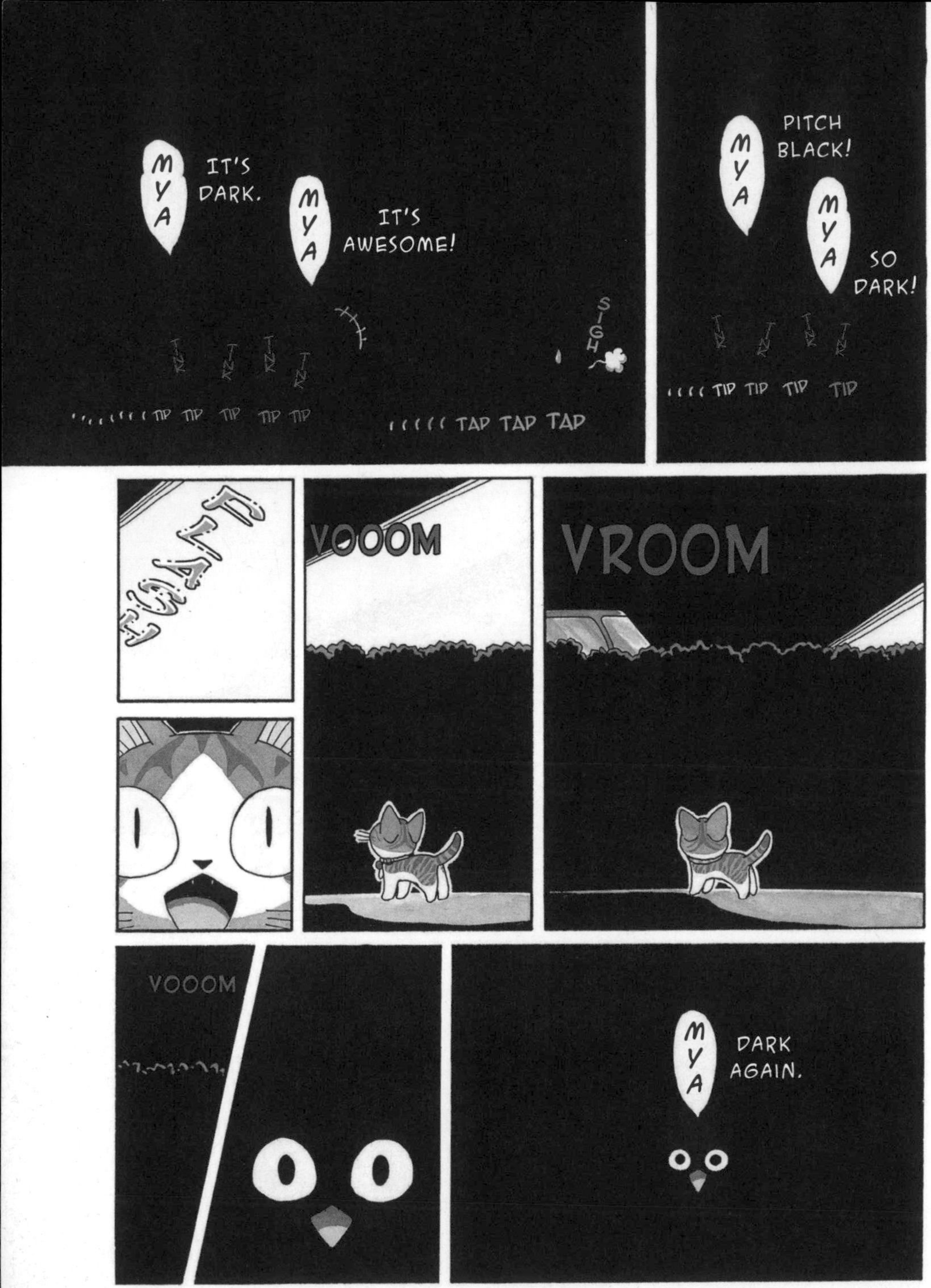
MYA
IT'S DARK.
MYA
IT'S AWESOME!
TINK TINK TINK TINK
TIP TIP TIP TIP TIP
TAP TAP TAP
SIGH
MYA
PITCH BLACK!
MYA
SO DARK!
TINK TINK TINK TINK
TIP TIP TIP TIP
FLASH
VOOOM
VROOM
VOOOM
MYA
DARK AGAIN.

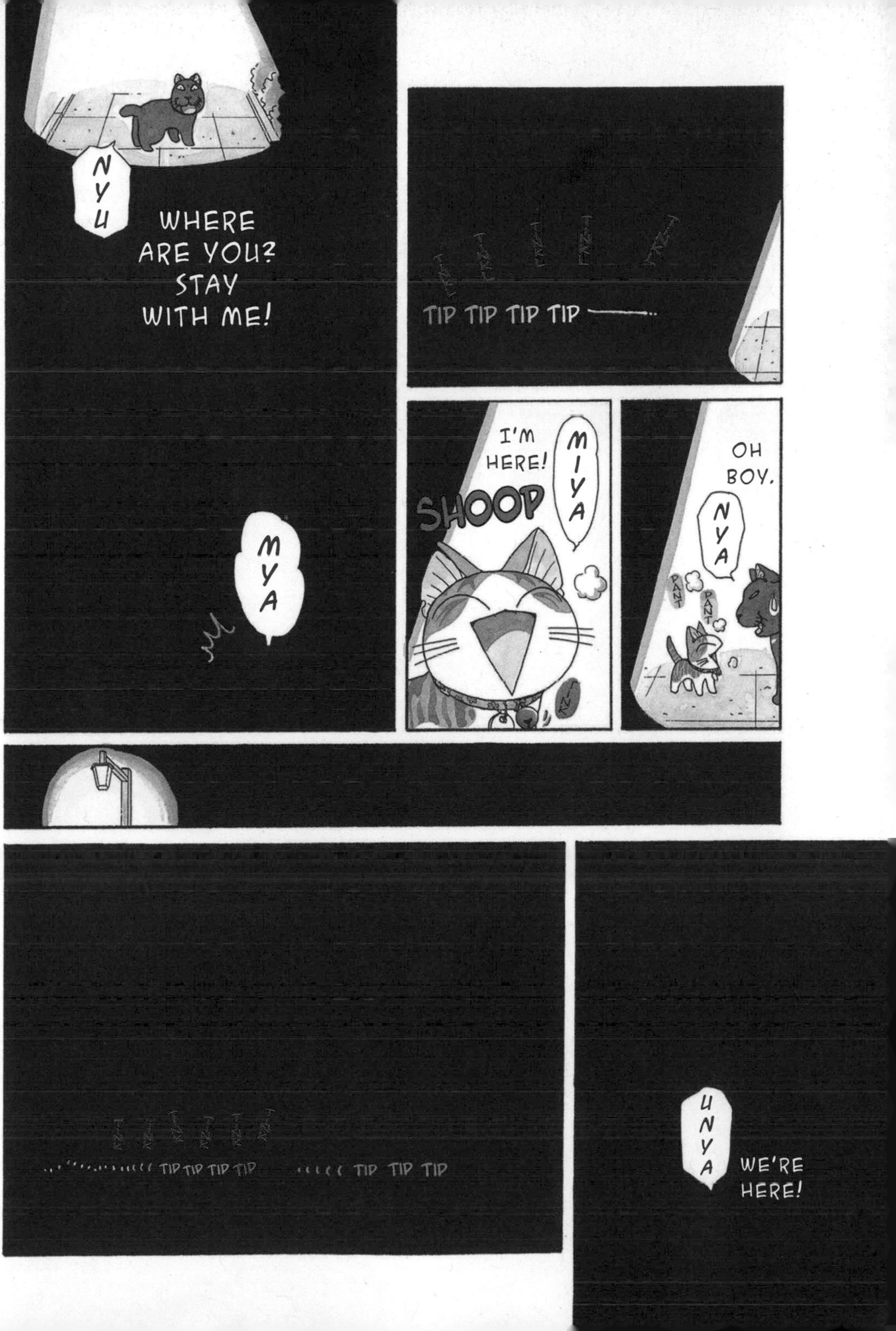
NYU
WHERE ARE YOU? STAY WITH ME!
MYA
TIP TIP TIP TIP
I'M HERE!
MIYA
SHOOP
OH BOY.
NYA
PANT
PANT
TIP TIP TIP TIP
TIP TIP TIP
UNYA
WE'RE HERE!

MYA
WHERE ARE WE?
STARE
OH!
MEOW!
IT'S THE PARK!

the end

homemade 109: a cat continues to saunter

TINK
TINK
TINK
TINK
TINK
TINK
TINK
TINK
TINK
TINK
FWIP
GLARE
FWIP
GLARE
?!

WHAT NOW?
WHAT'S GOING ON?
STARE
MEOW
SO MANY OF YOUS!

MYA
ARE THEY BLACKIE'S FRIENDS?
...NYU
YOU COULD SAY THAT.
ARE YA GONNA PLAY?
MIYA
BAMF
NYA
JUST STAY STILL FOR A MINUTE.
UNYA
IT'S AN IMPORTANT GATHERING.
YA AIN'T GONNA PLAY?
MEOW
HMMM
MEE
...

HUP
LET'S PLAY!
MEOW
SHFF SHFF SHFF
NYA
ENJOY THE CALM.
BAH
WELL, CHI'S GONNA TAKE A WALK IN THE PARK.
MIYA
DON'T GO TOO FAR, OKAY?
UNYA

TINK TINK TINK TINK TINK TINK TINK
MYA
WHAT'S THIS?
OH, IT'S THE WATERY PLACE!
TINK TINK TINK TINK
SKT SKT SKT
AH!
MYA
IT'S THE SANDY PLACE!
FIP FIP
MYA?
FIP FIP
WOW
MEOW
IT'S FLAP-FLAPPING!
NYUU
HMM?

FIP FIP
NYU...
FIP FIP
KREE--- KREE---
MYA

SOMETHING'S CHIRPING.
KREE KREE
KREE KREE
KREE KREE
KREE KREE
KREE KREE
KREE KREE

HUSH
...?

the end

homemade 110: a cat steps forth

SHMP
STARE
OH, IT'S THAT KID FROM BEFORE.

CHI
SLINK SLINK SLINK SLINK
TWINGE TWINGE TWINGE
FLEX
TINK TINK TINK TINK TINK TINK
HOP
HEY, WHAT YA UP TO?
MEOW
GRIN
TINK
!
MEOW
OH, PREY!
MIYA
ARE YOU PLAYING?
BOING BOING BOING

MIYA
MAY CHI PLAY TOO?
MGA
MYA
HRN?
MRR
THIS AIN'T NO GAME!
MERR
LEAVE ME ALONE.
TIP TIP TIP
CHI
TINK TINK TINK TINK TINK
TIP TIP TIP TIP
TIP TIP TIP TIP
TINK TINK TINK TINK TINK TINK TINK TINK TINK
TIP TIP TIP TIP
TIP TIP TIP TIP
HALT
...

ZIP
WHAT'S WITH THAT RIDICULOUS NOISE?!
MEWR
CHI
CHI DOESN'T KNOW.
MYA
BUT WE'RE FINE.
MYA
WE AIN'T! WE CAN'T HUNT LIKE THAT!
MRR
LET'S PLAY!
MEOW
WHERE ARE WE GOING?
MEOW
STOP FOLLOWING ME.
MERR
I'LL BE HEADING OFF TO A FUN PLACE NOW.
MERR

MRR
HRMPH!
TIP TIP TIP
TIP TIP TIP
DON'T GO TOO FAR, NOW.
NYAN
...TIP TIP TIP
TURN
MIYA
WAIT UP!
MERR
UGH!
DASH—
MIYA
WAIT!
DASH—
MEWR
DASH—
WOAH!
RUN AWAY!
MEWR
MIYA
WAIT FOR ME!

MRR
HUP
HOP
MEOW
YAY
HOP
MEOW MEOW
WHAT A BWAST!
YANK
GAK
HUH?
SNAG
?!
GAG !!

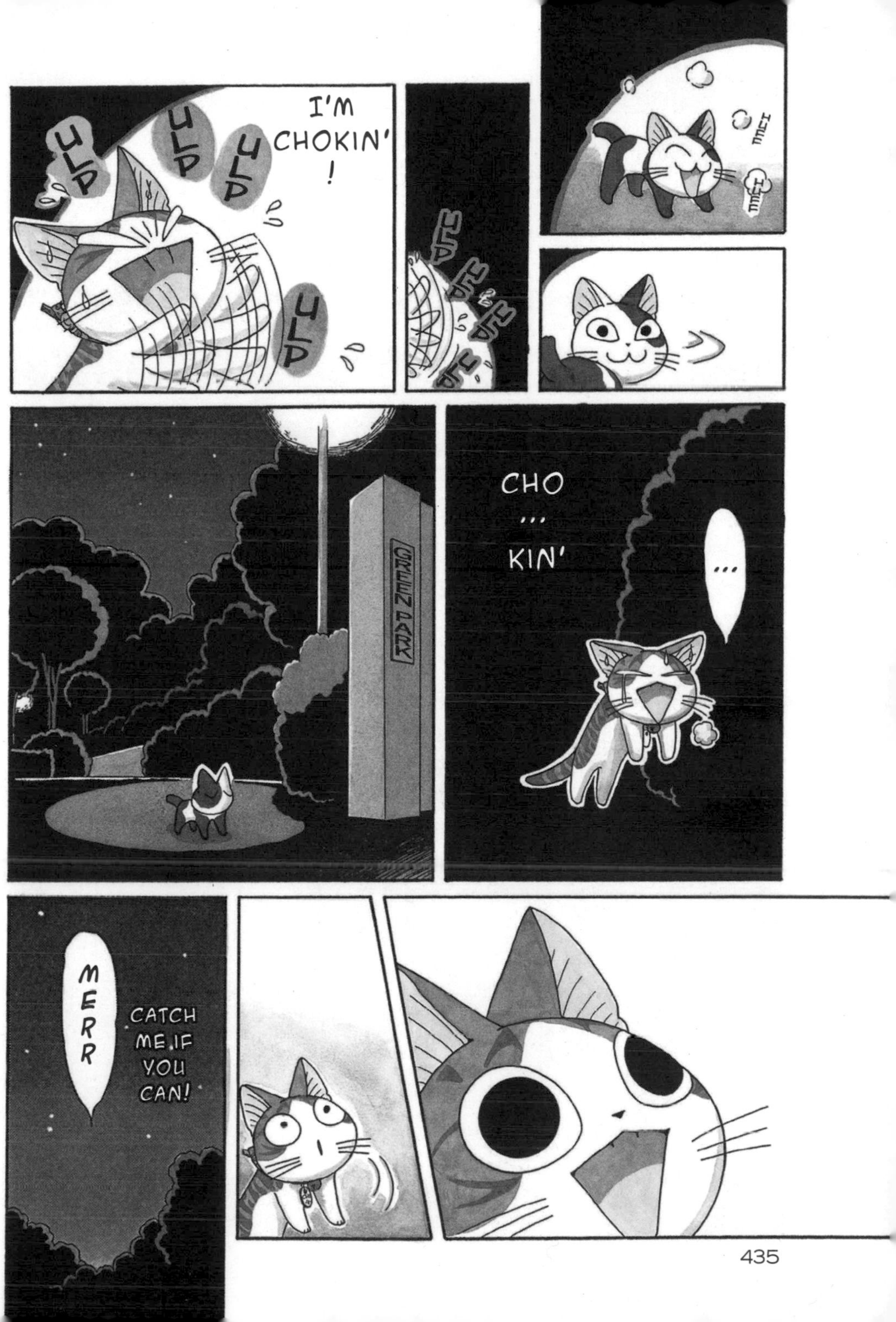

ULP
ULP
ULP
I'M CHOKIN'!
ULP
ULP ULP ULP
HEE HEE
CHO... KIN'
...
MERR
CATCH ME IF YOU CAN!

FLEX
CHI IS
MIYA
HERE TO PLAY!
SPROING
SNAP
CHI
CHI
MRR
MEOW
HA
HAH
HAH
HA
HAH
DASHI

the end

Special Collaboration Manga

TWO FUNNY FELINES CHI & KURO

Risa Ito
creator of "Oy, Pi-tan"

×

Konami Kanata
creator of "Chi's Sweet Home"

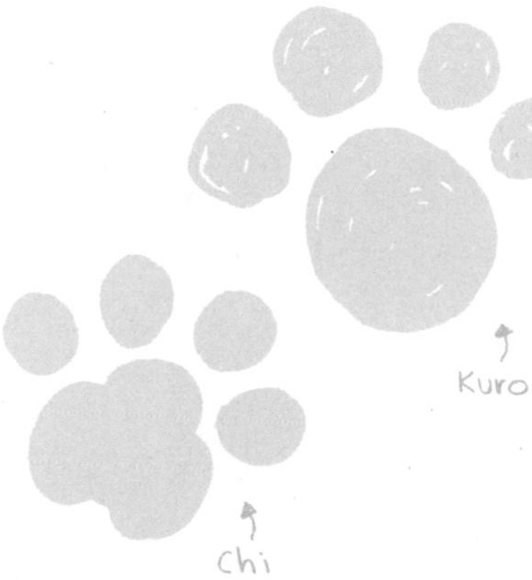
Kuro
Chi

HRN? IS THAT MS. KONAMI'S CHI OVER THERE?
MIU
MIU
HEY? IT'S MS. ITO'S KURO.
SHE WON THE *KODANSHA MANGA PWIZE, RIGHT?
Yeah, I won it. But it doesn't pay the bills.
*KODANSHA MANGA AWARD
*Says the cat, not us.
DID YOU KNOW THAT KONAMI KANATA WAS RISA ITO'S SENIOR IN HIGH SCHOOL?
TRUE
HEE! I-A-APOLO-GIZE!
MS. KO-NAMI!
GLAD TO BE IN MORNING!
She was also better at math.
Konami Knows Ito once received a zero on a test.

Stone and dirt
OH! MEAT!
IT'S MEAT!
THE CUTER ONE SHOULD
TILT
EAT FIRST, NO?
HEY YOU...
SHALL WE SAY THE ONE WITH MORE COLOR PAGES?
Or maybe...
This
CLAY (ITO)
PAINT (KONAMI)
New "Oy, Pi-tan" covers are photos of clay figures.
And they are really good!
"CHI'S SWEET HOME" VOLS. 1–11 ARE ALL ON SALE IN FULL COLOR!
O-OK, GO FIRST!!
VOLS 1–14 OF "OY, PI-TAN" ARE BEW AND ONLY ON SALE IN JAPAN.
The dirt is from kneeling down in apology...
Dirt
HRMPH!
BUT NONE OF THAT MATTERS TO US CATS!
IN OUR WORLD
SIZE IS WHAT COUNTS!
SAY,
TILT
DID YOU KNOW?
HMM?
C-Cute...
KONAMI KANATA'S FATHER IS A TEACHER, AND HE TOOK GOOD CARE OF RISA ITO WHEN SHE WAS IN GRADE SCHOOL.
EEK!
TRUE
Her mom and dad are both nice people, I hear.
HE WAS A GREAT HELP!
AND HOW IS MR. ICHIO DOING THESE DAYS?
They all say she's a "good girl." No wonder she's embarrassed.

SAY SUCH THINGS, AND ITO WILL DRAW CHI!
MI-GYA
POOF
TAKE THAT !!
Dirt, stone, and grass...
Chi as drawn by Ms. Ito.
CHI WANTS TO GO HOME!
SEE! EXPERIENCE ITO'S GREATNESS!
WHY AM I SO UGWY ?
NYA-HA-HA!
SWITCH ME BACK!
RIGHT BACK AT YA...
HRN?
POOF
Kuro as drawn by Ms. Konami.
KURO'S... GONNA STAY WITH MORNING!!
FAIL!
HEY YOU !!
HOW UTTERLY BEAUTIFUL!!
the end

Chi is also an anime!!

CSN
Chi's Sweet News

news special:
Chi has an anime and a website
THE CHI'S SWEET HOME ANIME IS AVAILABLE ON DVD AND STREAMING VIA CRUNCHYROLL!
www.crunchyroll.com
NYA
AND READERS CAN FIND CHI CALENDARS AND POSTERS AT www.chi-sweethome.tumblr.com
Konami Kanata
Blackie
CHI!
OH, THE EDITOR.
?
CHI, LET'S GO. HURRY!
?
HUH?

Congrats Chi's an Anime Again!!

CSN Chi's Sweet News

news special:

Chi once again adapted into an anime!

AFTER THE GREAT SUCCESS OF THE FIRST SERIES, CHI'S SWEET HOME WAS ADAPTED FOR YET ANOTHER SEASON! CHI'S NEW ADDRESS IS NOW ON DVD THROUGH DISCOTEK MEDIA!
www.discotekmedia.com
THIS SECOND SEASON STARTS WITH THE YAMADAS MOVING INTO THEIR NEW PET-FRIENDLY CONDO.
UNYA
Konami Kanata
Blackie
CHI'S GOTTA HURRY TO INFORM EVEWY-ONE!
DASH
MIW
I'LL BE MAKING AN APPEAR-ANCE AS WELL.
AT YOUR SERVICE.
NEXT!!
DASH
...
?
AS YOU SEE, THERE'LL BE A WIDE CAST!

Who knew these characters had such backgrounds...

In the anime's second season we get to meet many of Chi's new neighbors. So in this extra we'd like to share some character designs as well as profiles created for the anime. Once you know their personalities better, you might discover something new when you watch the anime.

Name: Yuki Kusano
Age: 12 years old
Family Structure: Lives with his mom and dad and older sister.
Personality: Energetic and good at sports (especially those involving a ball).

David and the Kusano Boy

Name: David
Gender: Male
Breed: Beagle
Age: About 6 months old
Caretakers: the Kusano family
Personality: Always full of spunk. And while he's got a silly side, he always loyally listens to the Kusano boy.

Name: Mee
Age: Unknown
Gender: Unknown
Breed: Holland Lop
Caretaker: Mr. Furukawa
Personality: Mysterious and always silent, Mee lives life at its own pace.

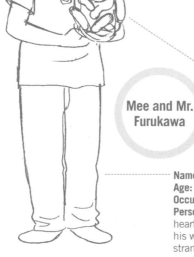

Mee and Mr. Furukawa

Name: Kazuya Furukawa
Age: 51 years old
Occupation: Advertising firm employee
Personality: Always heard laughing heartily. Enjoys traveling abroad with his wife, where he often purchases strange souvenirs.

MYA
IS THAT RIGHT...

Auntie Cali

Name: Cali
Gender: Female
Breed: Calico
Age: About 40 in human years
Caretakers: She lives in a large traditional Japanese home.
Personality: Often seen smiling, but she's also a little forgetful.

Alice and Saori

Name: Saori Ijuuin
Age: 26 years old
Occupation: Picture book author; her pen name is Yume Hanabatake
Personality: Gentle and calm, yet kinda ditzy.

Name: Alice
Gender: Female
Breed: Scottish Fold Longhair
Personality: Gentle and calm, yet kinda ditzy.
Age: 12 to 18 months
Caretaker: Saori
Personality: Very proud, but occasionally she succumbs to her feline nature.

Lucky & Mrs. Akashi

Name: Lucky
Gender: Male
Age: About 18 in human years
Caretaker: the Akashi family
Talents: He can mimic words.
Personality: He lacks the nervousness of other small birds and is quite bold.

Name: Yasuko Akashi
Age: In her 60's
Occupation: Housewife
Personality: Composed and big-hearted.

PLEASE ENJOY THE ANIME TOO!
MYA

First Look!

The World of *Chi's Sweet Home* finally revealed!

Ever wonder just how Chi's world really looks like? Or where the Mama's home is relative to the Yamadas' apartment? How about the distance from the Yamadas' to the park where Chi and Yohei met? Problem solved! With the following map, now you can properly figure out where the cast of *Chi's Sweet Home* live.

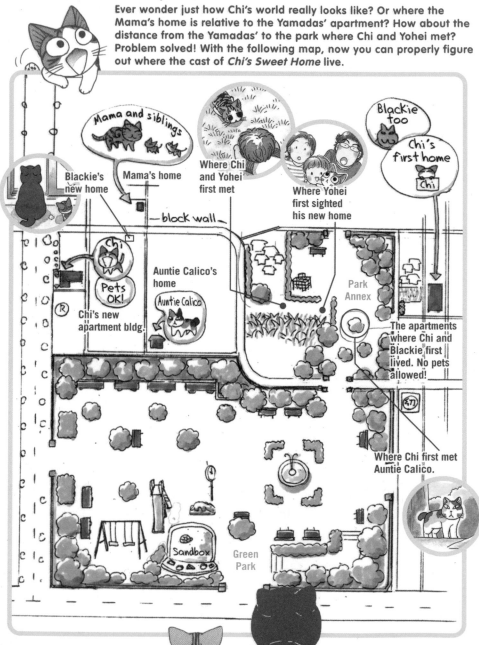

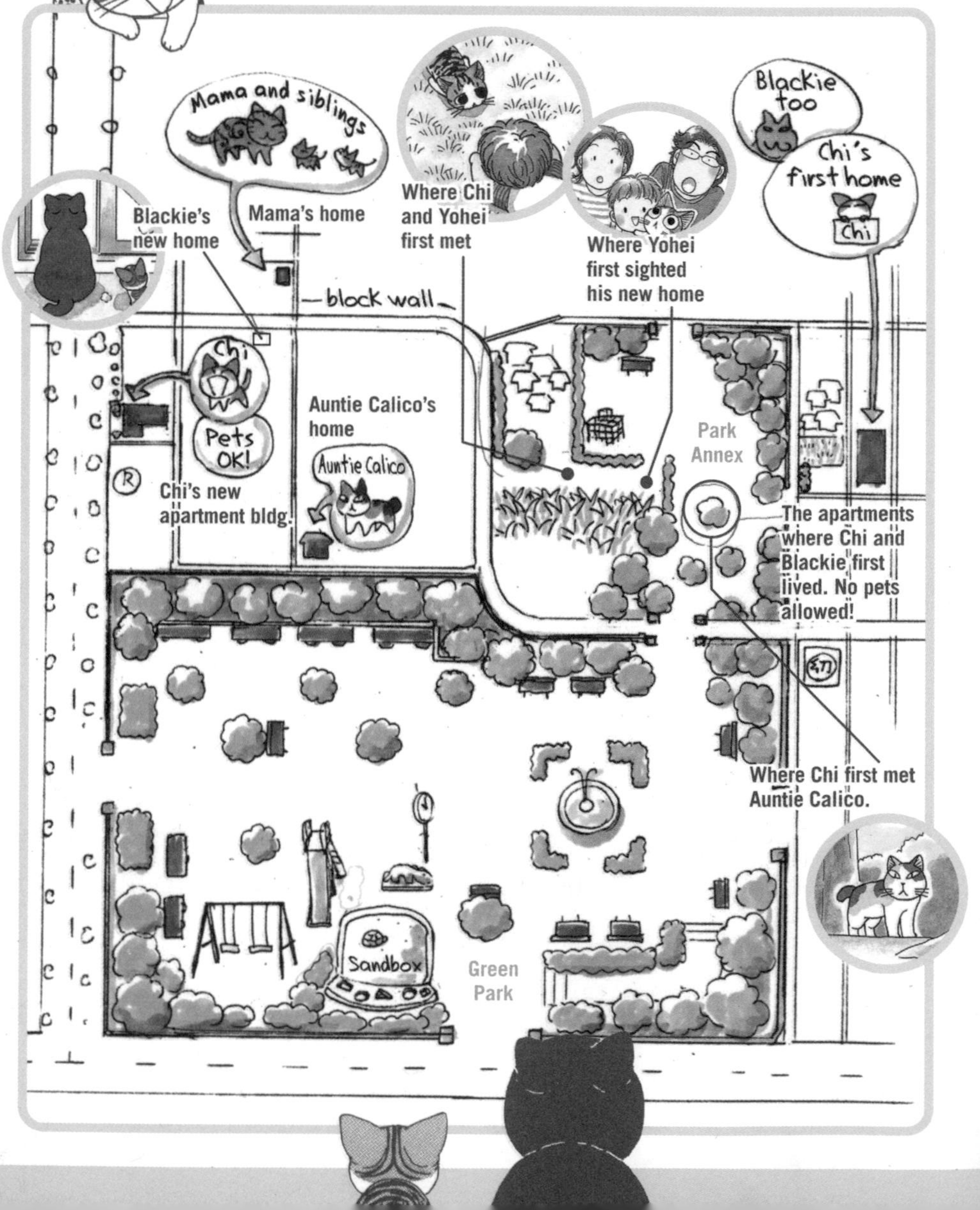
Mama and siblings
Mama's home
Blackie's new home
Where Chi and Yohei first met
Where Yohei first sighted his new home
Blackie too
Chi's first home
Chi
block wall
Chi
Pets OK!
Chi's new apartment bldg.
Auntie Calico's home
Auntie Calico
Park Annex
The apartments where Chi and Blackie first lived. No pets allowed!
Where Chi first met Auntie Calico.
Sandbox
Green Park

Chi's globe-trekking!

MYA

Chi's on tour!

Emboldened by her travels with her Japanese publisher Kodansha, Chi is now touring the U.S. Follow our cute kitty on her two websites as she travels the globe!

So far Chi has been to these locations!
Chi's Travel Map
FRANCE
Paris/Chablis/Beaujolais/Beaune
ITALY
Milano/Lucca/Vinci/Pisa/Firenze
Taichung/Hualien/Taipei
TAIWAN
Hong Kong/Macao
CHINA
AMERICA
Los Angeles/San Diego
New York
AMERICA
Chi's Sweet

Beaune
strolling through Château Clos de Vougeot

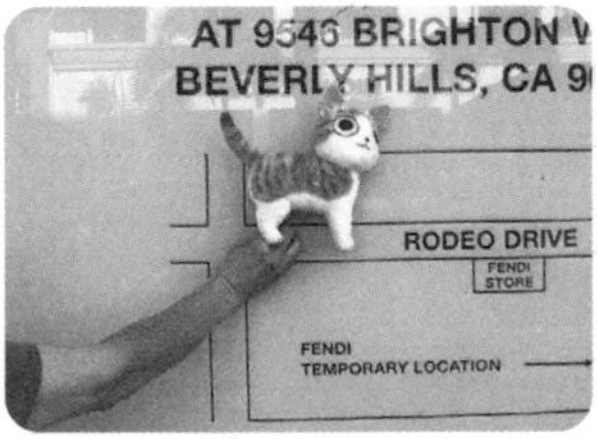
AT 9546 BRIGHTON W
BEVERLY HILLS, CA 9
RODEO DRIVE
FENDI STORE
FENDI TEMPORARY LOCATION

Los Angeles
shopping on Rodeo Drive

Macao
view from the Ruins of St. Paul's

Taipei
at Xingtian Temple

Lucca
view from Guinigi Tower

New York
encounter on Brooklyn Bridge

NYAN

These are just a few of the photos available.
Please head on to the sites for more.

Web URLs:

www.chisweethome.net (English)

http://morningmanga.com/chisweetravel/ (Japanese)

YOU'RE WRONG!
NOW YOU'VE DONE IT
DON'T MESS WITH ME
MYA
MRRR
MEOWR
MERRR
MEOWR
YOU'RE JUST A "LI'L KITTY"!
GET OUT OF HERE!
I'M NOT A "KITTY"
MEOW
MERR
MEWRR

CHI & COCCHI

Leave as friends, return as frenemies ♥

The tale of these two li'l beasties continues in Part 3!

Practicing with the Scratching Post

FUKU FUKU
SHFF
PET SHO
ITCHY
ITCHY
ITCHY
ITCHY
ITCHY
ITCHY
MEEE!
GRAAH

SKFF
KLAW KLAW KLAW
AH!
SHFF
FUKUFUKU, USE THIS SCRATCHING POST TO SHARPEN YOUR CLAWS, OK?
Scratch Post
MEE?
OH, MY.
TIP TIP TIP

MEEEE!
KLAW KLAW KLAW
AAH!
YOINK
DROP
DO THAT HERE, OK?
MEE?

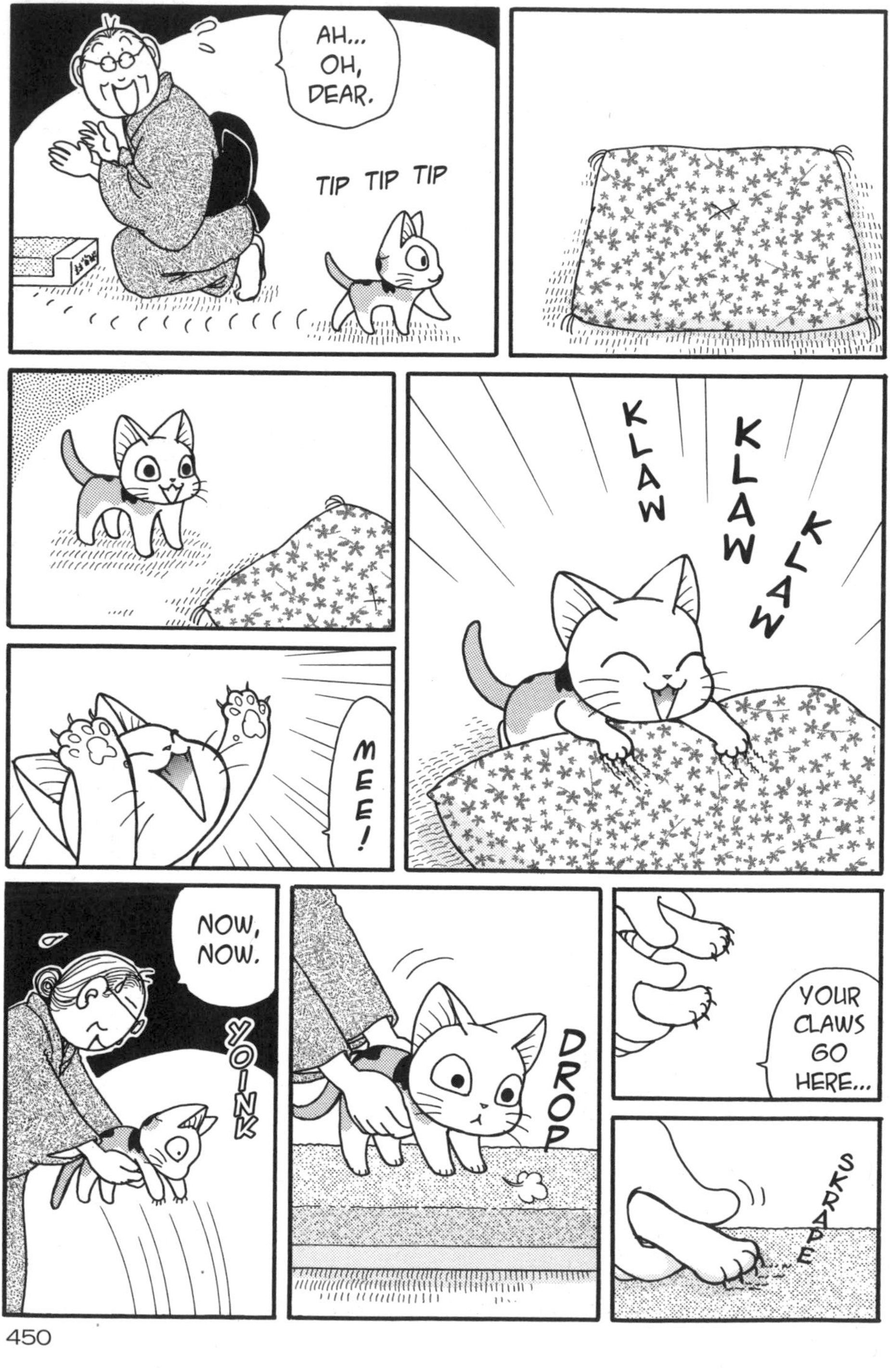
AH... OH, DEAR.
TIP TIP TIP
KLAW KLAW KLAW
MEE!
NOW, NOW.
YOINK
DROP
YOUR CLAWS GO HERE...
SKRAPE

SO YOU CAN SHARPEN THEM.
SEE?
SKRAPE SKRAPE
YES! THAT'S IT!
GRAB
MEE!
GOOD JOB! YOU DID IT!
MEE?
SKTT SKTT SKTT

WHIPP
KLAW
MEE!
WHIPP
... ...
KLAW
KLAW
KLAW
KLAW
KLAW

the end

FUKU
FUKU

WOOW

Kitten's Grand Adventure
FUKU FUKU
RUSTLE
MEE.
TIP TIP TIP
TIP TIP TIP
TIP TIP TIP

SHFF
SHFF
SHFF
SHFF
NMEE?
BZZZ
BZZZZ
ZISH
LOOOM
!

MEEE
SKAMPER
haa
haa
PANT
haa
PANT
PANT
haa
LOOOOM
PANT
PANT
PANT
MEE?
MEE!
SKAMPER
MEEE!
haa
haa

haah
MEE.
SKFF
SKFF
MEW.
SKFF
SKFF
MEEEE!
MEW!
MRM?
LOOOOOM
MEEEE!

MEEEE!
MEWW!
MEW!
MEEEE!
MEEEE!
MEE?
BRRNYA?
...
...
YOINK
MEEE!
GLANCE GLANCE
IT'S HARD TO FIND YOU 'CAUSE YOU'RE SO SMALL.
FUKU-FUKU!
FUKU-FUKU!

OH!
A CAT!
HOW NOW?
MEW MEW!
MEE MEE!
FOUND YOU!
THANKS FOR SHOWING ME THE WAY.
BRRNYA?
MEE

the end

The Complete
Chi's Sweet Home, Part 2

Translation - Ed Chavez
Marlaina McElheny
Production - Grace Lu
Hiroko Mizuno
Glen Isip
Tomoe Tsutsumi

First published in Japan in 2007, 2008, 2009 by Kodansha, Ltd., Tokyo
Publication for this English edition arranged through Kodansha, Ltd., Tokyo
English language version produced by Vertical Comics,
an imprint of Kodansha USA Publishing, LLC

Published by of Kodansha USA Publishing, LLC, New York

Originally published in Japanese as *Chiizu Suiito Houmu 4-6* by Kodansha, Ltd., 2007-2009
Chiizu Suiito Houmu first serialized in *Morning*, Kodansha, Ltd., 2004-2015

FukuFuku: Kitten Tales chapters 10 and 11 originally published in Japanese as *FukuFuku Funya~n Ko-neko da Nyan* by Kodansha, Ltd., 2014
FukuFuku Funya~n Ko-neko da Nyan first serialized in *Be Love*, Kodansha, Ltd., 2013-2015

ISBN: 978-1-942993-17-9

Manufactured in Canada

First Edition

Seventh Printing

Kodansha USA Publishing, LLC
451 Park Avenue South, 7th Floor
New York, NY 10016
www.kodansha.us

Special thanks to K. Kit[illegible]

Vertical books are distributed through Penguin-Random House Publisher Services.